COUNTDOWN TO RETIREMENT

Harry Miller

COUNTDOWN TO RETIREMENT

Hutchinson Benham
London

Hutchinson Benham Limited
3 Fitzroy Square, London W 1 P 6JD

An imprint of the Hutchinson Group

London Melbourne Sydney Auckland
Wellington Johannesburg and agencies
throughout the world

First published 1978
© ♺ National Westminster Bank Limited 1978

Set in Monotype Joanna
Printed in Great Britain by The Anchor Press Ltd
and bound by Wm Brendon & Son Ltd
both of Tiptree, Essex

ISBN 0 09 133491 8

Contents

PART ONE

Preparing for Retirement

I

A New Outlook

The word 'retired' has undergone a subtle change over the years. A generation ago, when people now retiring started work, it had a class connotation. A retired man was one who had been in a fairly well-paid job or self-employed, and had saved enough to live on without further earning. If he had been a Civil Servant or a schoolmaster, his income was supplemented with a professional pension. He was middle class, comfortable and respected.

But there were other retired people to whom that dignified classification did not apply. They were a much more numerous but much less exalted class, distinguished from the élite retired with the name of old age pensioner. In the strict sense of the term they were no less retired than the ex-Civil Servant or business manager. Like him they had worked all their lives and had come to the inevitable divide. But there were social and financial differences. He could afford leisure, they had a struggle. He had money, they received 'charity'.

In fact, the old age pension was not a charity. The intention behind it was the same as it is today. It was the community's recognition that something was still owing to those who had worked for half a century and had nothing to show for it. For many reasons, political as well as humane, worn-out workers could not be left completely destitute.

Yet, though not a charity, the pension smelt of charity. The odour of the discarded but not forgotten Poor Law hung over the recipients. There was a further stigma in the form of national assistance, for which the poor could apply when their resources fell to starvation level. Retired people, so-called, could not qualify – did not want to qualify – for the old age pension, and never needed to seek national assistance. So those who were old and poor did not retire; they were swept on to a slightly softened scrap heap.

Nothing shows more vividly the changed concept of retirement in recent years than the modifications in terminology. Old habits and the prejudices that inspire them die hard, and people are still often called old age pensioners. But officially at least the old age pension no longer exists. It has become a retirement pension. The retired now encompass the whole income span, from the poorest to millionaires. National assistance has also been tactfully renamed. It is now a supplementary pension.

A kind of means test still remains, based on earnings. Men are entitled to receive the retirement pension at sixty-five and women at sixty. But for the first five pensionable years it is subject to reductions in respect of earnings over a certain figure, which is increased from time to time as inflation diminishes the value of the concession. After the five-year gap the pension becomes a straight addition to income, subject to income tax like any other earnings.

That is, at the age of seventy for men and sixty-five for women, no one is too rich to qualify for the national retirement pension. Most of the rich probably take it. When Mr Harold Macmillan turned seventy he was photographed for the Press drawing his first week's pension at a post office. It was a deliberate gesture in support of the new attitude. It indicated that there was no shame attached to the receipt of the state pension. It was everyone's right, a classless privilege.

With the social upgrading of the pension, the old age pensioner has been dignified with a new name. He and she are now 'senior citizens'. The term is perhaps an over-compensation. It has the merit of sounding respectful and is consistent with the new retirement image. There may be other distinctions among senior citizens, but the new retirement dispensation has been a great leveller.

State pensioners have acquired more self-respect along with the respect of others. They are better off, better dressed, and more self-assured than in the past. The hangdog look has gone. They claim their pension as a due and not as supplicants. Officials are kinder in their treatment of the old, more tolerant of ignorance and bewilderment, more patient in elucidating rules and regulations.

New ideas about egalitarianism in our society may have had something to do with the change. The former social gap between clerical and manual work, professional and commercial jobs, salaries and wages, has narrowed almost to vanishing point. Retired people of all kinds draw their pensions at the post office as nonchalantly as, if with less panache than, Mr Macmillan. People with concessionary bus passes are, age apart, indistinguishable from the paying passengers.

Most people really need these concessions. Inflation nibbles at every increase in the pension and every additional item of welfare from the moment it is granted. (The financial problems of retirement and advice on ways of dealing with them are discussed at length in Part Three of this book). But the overall picture is brightening as governments try to ease the burden of rising costs. For many years up to the second world war the old age pension was 10/– (50p) a week. Even if that sum is grossed up to present day inflated values it is infinitely smaller than even the most docile of today's poor would tolerate. A turning point came with Sir William (later Lord) Beveridge's recommendation in 1942 of an improved scheme of social insurance, which was implemented soon after World War II ended. That was the start of the new conception of retirement which has made its biggest advances in the 1970s.

PENSIONERS HAVE BECOME IMPORTANT

There are pressing reasons for the recent acceleration of reform. One of them is a genuine upsurge of sympathy with the old, and especially of concern for the aged poor. Another is prompted by a sense of shame with the realization that our standards of living and of social security, once among the highest in the world, are now below those of many of our partners in the European Community. A third motive is political expediency. Governments are anxiously aware of the imbalance of our population. The old are increasing in numbers at a faster rate than the population as a whole. We shall continue to have an ageing population.

Statistics show that the proportion of people over sixty-five in this country has more than doubled since the beginning of the century. It rises every year. In 1970 it was 12.8 per cent of the population; in 1976, 13.8 per cent. The over-sixty-fives are now nearly one-seventh of Britain's fifty-six million people. Eight million adults are a force, whether they exercise force or not.

Our senior citizens are never likely to become an organized lobby. But they are a kind of passive lobby, second in size only to the equally unorganized multitude of housewives (with whom of course they overlap). Though passive and without corporate power, the sheer numbers of the retired make them politically formidable. Not that the politicians need fear belligerent demonstrations from this most law-abiding section of the community. But they have reason to take account of the fact that even a minority of the over-sixties could be numerous enough to sway an election.

Trade unions are also alert to the tactical importance of the nation's pensioners. Millions of them were once union members, and millions of existing members are near enough to retirement to be concerned about their prospects. In demanding bigger retirement pensions the unions feel they are serving their members' interests no less than by urging wage increases and reduction of unemployment.

The public as well as the authorities are taking more interest in their retired members. This is partly because the old are too numerous to be ignored, and because their claims are more strongly publicized than in the past, but also because they are becoming much more active in the community. In fact, the old are getting younger.

Most of us remember what our grandparents were like at today's normal retirement age. It was not simply that they looked very old to our young eyes. Family albums show them at sixty-odd looking as old as people ten to fifteen years older do now. Grandpa was elderly at fifty and worn out by the time he gave up work. If he lived into his eighties he was a local phenomenon. Life was no doubt harder. It was certainly shorter.

At the beginning of the century expectation of life at birth was forty-six for men and fifty for women. By mid-century it had risen to sixty-six and seventy-three. Today a newborn baby boy can expect to live to sixty-nine and a girl to over seventy-five. The heartening fact about life figures is, of course, that they are progressive. The longer we live, the longer we can expect to live beyond the initial statistical forecast. Life expands for the retired.

The social services are largely responsible. The National Health Service has made it possible for people, no matter how poor they might be, to seek medical help when necessary and to benefit from what might otherwise have been prohibitively expensive treatment. Thanks to improved medical facilities and skills some of the old killer diseases such as tuberculosis have been virtually eliminated, and even cancer in some of its forms can be successfully treated.

Improvements in the standard of living have ensured that people on the whole are better fed, clothed and housed. There is still a long way to go. Society has no right to be complacent about its achievements in welfare. But there is living proof of how much has been accomplished.

As one would expect, the improvement is mental as well as physical. Fitness and the prospect of longer life are great stimulants to healthy thinking and activity. That is why books are written to help the elderly make the best use of their retirement, for their own sakes and the community's.

There is a noticeable trend among older people towards a youthful outlook. People are considered youngish who, only a few decades ago, would have been labelled middle-aged. Women who would have concealed their age from thirty onwards are now often willing to admit to the forties if only for the satisfaction of being told, 'I can't believe it!'

Deferred ageing should logically result in deferred retirement by keeping people fit for work longer. It was paradoxical therefore that there should be a movement in the mid 1970s in favour of earlier retirement. It is still in the discussion stage, and it may take many years to overcome the obstacles. But there seems to be no doubt that more people will opt for more leisure and an earlier pension to enjoy it.

Life tables show women to be the stronger sex

The idea has received some trade unions support. Workers in the most exacting jobs want release from physical strain before they become too old to bear it without permanent injury to health. Coal-miners and blast-furnacemen have begun to campaign strongly for early retirement. So far the arguments have been in respect of physical strain. But there are other kinds of strain. Bus drivers in congested streets, policemen in an increasingly lawless society, business executives in fiercely competitive economic conditions, can put up a convincing case for earlier retirement. And they probably will.

Some unions see early retirement as a means of releasing jobs for the unemployed. Employers, on the other hand, might find it helpful in reducing over-manning and speeding up promotion. There have been suggestions, strongly opposed by women wage-earners, that in the interests of sexual equality, and because the life tables show women to be the stronger sex, the woman's pensionable age should be raised to sixty-five. The most likely event will be a phased reduction of the men's retirement age to a standard sixty for both sexes.

The main difficulties are, of course, financial. Estimates of cost to the State of paying retirement pensions to everyone at sixty vary between £1000 million and £2000 million a year. Industrial pension schemes would have to be re-drafted. Would companies dare to reduce the occupational pension by cutting the working span by five years? And suppose voluntary retirement before sixty becomes feasible; how will pensions be adjusted to satisfy both employer and pensioner?

The option to retire voluntarily in one's fifties may come sooner than we expect, despite the problems. It could make a big change in the pattern of retirement. Apart from a few special cases – for instance, men and women who have served in enervating tropical climates – people have always been elderly on retirement. But retirement at fifty-five, or even fifty, with an occupational pension will bring many people in the prime of life into the general ranks of the retired. Some may seek another full-time career in employment, or become self-employed, or find satisfactory leisure pursuits to occupy their twenty or more years expectation of life.

Choosing when to retire, with the employer's encouragement, has attractions for both sides. It will offer new freedoms, loosen old compulsions, perhaps create unfamiliar problems. The possibilities will be discussed in another chapter.

For the present, pensioned retirement remains at sixty-five and sixty, with perhaps, within a few years, the prospect of a reduction of the men's retirement age to sixty-four or sixty-three. How retirement looks to people in these age groups, how they can live happily and usefully throughout all the years to come, must be our next consideration.

2

Facing the Problems

While your retirement is still a fairly distant prospect – say fifteen or twenty years away – it often looks like a golden age. If your job is going badly, as all jobs do sometimes, retirement promises a blessed release. How often have we heard colleagues exclaiming, 'I'll be glad when I can retire and be rid of the monotony – the bullying – the rat race.'

But as retirement comes nearer, say within two or three years, the mood changes. It still promises escape, but anxiety, even fear, creeps in. You begin to wonder how you will manage on less money, how you will fill your time, how much you will miss the satisfactions of the job.

Both moods are misleading. No one knows what retirement will be like till it comes. Like marriage, retirement is an entirely new experience, for which your past experience, or your observation of other people's, has not prepared you. The fact that old J looks happy and old K is in despair may have no bearing on your own case. If you know something of their circumstances, you may find a few clues and learn some useful lessons. But you still have to live with, and become reconciled to, your new life.

Every case is in many respects unique. It presents individual problems, arising out of characteristics and conditions peculiar to yourself. But the uniqueness is in the detail, not in the broad picture. There are common problems which general experience can help to clarify and sometimes solve.

The transition from full-time paid occupation to full-time do-what-you-like-with-your-life is nearly always abrupt. There are exceptions. Some self-employed persons, especially freelance craftsmen such as journalists, house decorators, musicians and tree pruners, can reduce progressively the number of jobs they accept and pass imperceptibly into retirement. Some of these do not retire at all, till extreme age and infirmity make it impossible to hold a brush or tap the keys.

Some employers cushion the shock of retirement by reducing working hours and the work load for employees nearing the end of their career. This practice of phased retirement will no doubt spread. It is not pure benevolence. It helps to remove the difficulty of retaining the older workers within the system when their mental and physical slow-down might impede the general effort. Employees welcome the reduction of pressure. But such policies do not prevent retirement from being sudden and disturbing. Up to your last Friday you are a member of a team and the organization to which it belongs. Then come the goodbyes and good wishes, perhaps a cash-lined handshake, and the cord is severed. On Monday you are on your own.

To some it feels like the end of their world. They knew it had to come, but were afraid to think of it. Like a surgical operation or an accident, it was something that happened to other people. They had not fully realized up to the last Friday how old they had become. After all, they were still employable. Now they look in the mirror and see a face that shows every day of sixty-five.

It is impossible to guess how many people take that bleak view of retirement. We hope very few do. Most of us are a mixture of optimism and pessimism. Whether we feel free or adrift, elated or downcast, depends on how we face the new situation.

How successfully one faces retirement bears no relation to social position, education, affluence or the nature and status of the former job. It is linked to temperament, adaptability, *savoir faire* and breadth of interests. A retired senior executive may be at a loss; a labourer may have looked forward eagerly to the day when he could give more time to his vegetable-growing and photography.

Accepting retirement is harder for those whose job has been their life's interest. They are mostly people in senior positions, who have helped to build up an enterprise. They are reluctant to leave long-term projects unfinished, and see others inherit what they have created. Having been wedded to a job, they find retirement a bereavement. Retirement is easiest for those who were not too deeply involved, emotionally and vocationally, in their jobs.

It is important not to be daunted by the prospect of retirement. Some misgivings are understandable. You may have heard of men who did not long survive the loss of a regular job. They aged quickly and died of boredom. You may remember having seen, on a seaside holiday, an elderly man drifting from one promenade shelter to another, retired amid plenty, but bewildered and unhappy. You should have said, There but for the grace of God and my native good sense go I.

Common sense suggests acceptance of what is one of the inexorable facts of life. Apart from the few who die in harness, we must all retire eventually. Just as we don't last for ever, so we don't remain fully active to the end. If health does not force the issue, society does, by fixing a pensionable age and so permitting employers to trim the employee ranks with a kind of rough justice. Since there is no sensible alternative, one has to be reconciled to the compulsions of age and social policy.

The more depressing thoughts about retirement remain in abeyance during the euphoric weeks immediately following upon the event. You feel liberated, in holiday mood, without the obligation to return to the grindstone. It is a good idea to suit the action to the mood and go away for a holiday. A change of scene inhibits brooding and prepares your mind for a clearer outlook on what lies ahead.

LOSSES AND GAINS

It would be foolish to pretend that, apart from the regular pay packet, nothing one values is lost by retirement. You miss the routine. Consciously you may often have chafed against it, but subconsciously you may have welcomed the regulation and stability it provided. The obligation to rise at a regular time, arrive at office or factory on time, and work to a schedule, were valuable disciplines. The weekend was all the more pleasant for what the working week exacted in physical and nervous energy. You felt you earned your relaxation.

Routine is good for morale. It keeps the spirit in trim just as exercise tones the muscles. We have all seen, and many of us know from experience, the deterioration that sets in after long unemployment. It is not immediately apparent to people about to retire that if one is not careful, retirement can become an indefinitely prolonged unemployment. The lesson is clear. Retirement can be demoralizing or stimulating according to how we use it.

There is a strong temptation to cut loose from discipline. Retirement is an invitation to that form of self-indulgence. In moderation, self-indulgence is one of the joys of life. It would be hard indeed if we could not permit ourselves some freedom from restraint after forty or fifty years of taking instructions and receiving kicks for lapses in performance. A retired man is his own master, usually for the first time in his life. He may be softer than the master from whom he has just parted, but he must beware of killing the new one with too much kindness.

Where do you draw the line? Everyone must make his own decisions and organize a pattern of life that suits him. The key word is organize. Some people like a strict routine and are more severe with themselves than any boss has been. Their lives are almost mechanized. Retirement holds no snares for them. It is the people they live with who suffer.

The opposite type is much more common. Their time is now their own, so they believe they can afford to waste it. There is no pressing job to get up for, so they lie in bed till mid-morning and slop around the house all day in dressing gown and slippers. They are disorganized, indecisive, less happy than the rigid disciplinarians. And just as difficult to live with.

Lolling around in a dressing gown

Somewhere there is a happy mean, which you have to locate for yourself. Unless you are naturally an early riser you can afford to sleep later than your job allowed. But your life needs definition. Regular employment provides a clear-cut day and a sharply defined working week. In retirement the days can become shapeless and the distinction between week days and weekends blurred. Almost unawares, laxness can overtake you like a paralysis.

In those circumstances you tend to overdo the obvious and therefore effortless occupations. The most obvious and least exacting is watching television. It is a delightful entertainment and above all a blessing for the old and retired. But it should be part of a full life; otherwise it becomes a drug. A later chapter will offer suggestions for introducing variety into leisure and avoiding addictive traps.

A feature of employment that is lost through retirement is the companionship of the job. Members of an organization may not necessarily work as a team but they constitute a social unit. The sense of belonging is a team product. Discussing the job, the management and union matters, arguing about public issues, exchanging views on television programmes, are part of a community life which is cut off by retirement. You can no longer talk shop when the shop is closed to you. You cease to take part in the company's entertainments and societies. You can join the company's pensioners' association and enjoy its parties and outings, but that underlines your separation from the main stream of business life.

The human relationships of the place of work rarely overflow into the home. Most employed people lead a double life: one in the family circle and the other in the office or factory. When you retire one of these lives ends.

Even if you continue to meet old colleagues, you cannot participate in their parochial interests. A business is an organism and its activities develop and change. You learn about the changes as an outsider. Meeting people who are still involved can be depressing. It emphasizes the fact that you are out of touch. It should at the same time do something more positive, namely emphasize the need to seek new contacts and interests in place of the old. Life needs replenishing to make retirement enjoyable.

Among the intangible assets of an employed person is the status and identity that attach to a job. You have been an engineer, a superviser, a bricklayer, a shop assistant, an accountant. What are you now? Something with an 'ex-' in front of it? That is a negative attitude. It conveys a sense of demotion. It suggests that you have left a lot of self-respect behind with the job. Successful retirement is largely a state of mind. It is a challenge to acquire a new identity.

One of the main disabilities of living in the past is that it makes you unfit to live with in the present and future. Unless you live alone and have no human contacts – a rare case fortunately – there is one person who is very closely concerned in your retirement. Your wife.

WIVES AND RETIREMENT

Advisers on how to be happy though retired often tend to overlook or give only a perfunctory glance at the claims of the partner in the event. Yet most retired men are married, and no member of a team of two can retire alone. This does not mean that a wife retires when her husband does. Some wives would say their work increases. A husband at home all day has to be fed all day. He wants a sit-down midday meal whereas the wife has probably been in the habit of snatching a bite on the job. Now she has to deputize for the firm's canteen. She discovers that catering for two between breakfast and supper is not as simple as for one.

Formal retirement is for husbands, not for housewives. Perhaps that is why wives figure so slightly in discussions and plans on retirement. Cooking, cleaning, dealing with tradesmen, and all the accounting and managerial tasks of running a home continue whether or not the man of the house goes out to work. But life is not the same in every respect for the wife when her husband retires. She is caught up inevitably in the financial, emotional and operational effects of retirement. She is a partner in a situation which makes new demands of adjustment and co-operation on both concerned.

Many wives dread their husband's retirement. 'What will he do with himself?' they wonder. If he has few interests outside his paid work, or his interests are of a kind that will not fill his leisure, they visualize him hanging around the kitchen, getting in the way, becoming querulous and irritable. Even if the fears prove to be groundless, they are symptoms of a defect in far too many marriages, a defect of communication. They reveal that husband and wife have never discussed anything more personal than the household budget and the children's schooling. Millions of wives are vague about their husband's work and completely ignorant of how much he earns.

Apparently marriages can hold together even though husband and wife lead, mentally, separate lives. His job is outside the home and yields a weekly quantum of money. If decisions are required he makes them. It is only when a crisis arises that this way of life is seen to be inadequate. Retirement can be one of those crises.

The problems of retirement are resolved most satisfactorily where husband and wife have always talked things over. In other cases the adjustment will be difficult. There may even be some embarrassment. A man who has never thought of taking his wife into his counsel will have to face the fact that she can no longer be excluded. There will be money to discuss, ways and means to be contrived, two lots of pensions plus savings to be weighed against the missing earnings, a life-style to be modified or changed radically. One does not have to be an extreme feminist to recognize the right of a wife to an equal voice in so crucial a situation as retirement.

It is a mistake to postpone the discussions till the date of retirement. There is a great deal to decide and agreement takes time. In households that have always been ruled by a dominant male it will take longer to arrive at a new understanding than in those where both have always contributed to decision-making. Sudden transition from authoritarian to democratic government is as much a strain in families as in nations. In all cases, not excluding the democracies, it is advisable to start talking about retirement long before the date. That is one of the requirements of the advance planning which is being increasingly recommended to everyone who will one day retire.

Housewives cannot be said to retire unless they have been in paid employment. We shall not call them working wives; the implied distinction would offend all those women whose domestic work is never done. There are nine million women in paid employment, and hundreds of thousands, married, single or widowed, continue till retirement age. They face many but not all of the problems of men in retirement. Unmarried women and widows have to contend with loneliness, just as old bachelors and widowers do, but they cope better on the whole than men. Most men lack the domestic skills which provide women with a regular activity. Men have to seek some other anchor to avoid drifting in retirement. But there seem to be psychological as well as practical differences. Women are perhaps more self-contained and resourceful.

Retirement inflicts the heaviest deprivations on a man living alone. They are heaviest of all if he has been with the same firm for most of a working lifetime. People who have moved around are philosophical about change and competent in handling it. For loners who have grown into the job, retirement is like an amputation. In their case preparing well ahead for retirement can be a life-saver.

We have dwelt at some length on the dark side of retirement because it is the problems that make the initial impact. The compensations are easier to appreciate when you have got the measure of the problems. What you gain can balance and even outweigh the losses.

The immediate gain is an easier life. From the sixties onwards, or even before, muscles and nerves weaken but the rigours of the job do not diminish. The journey to and from work lengthens the working day and becomes more and more of a strain. Ageing manual workers and managers admit that they finish the daily stint too tired for anything more strenuous than television. Going out to a cinema or theatre or even the club requires an effort. Retirement brings sudden release from the pressures, the worry, the boredom and the sheer fatigue of the job. It feels like a miracle. It is probably an illusory escape. Life in retirement contains its own stresses, as we have seen. But they are not imposed by the powers outside.

If we make judicious use of the new freedom and resist the temptation to yield to a demoralizing idleness, we can recoup some of the strength spent in the last tough years of full-time employment. At sixty-plus, men and women in reasonable health are more resilient than is generally realized. It is not uncommon for retired people to say that they feel better than they have done for years.

In addition to ease, retirement provides time. A third of every day, which had been leased for half a lifetime to a succession of employers, is now your own to spend as you wish. Things you had always wanted to do and had no time for now become possible. It is an encouraging thought that one can have more time in one's sixties than one had twenty years earlier. Energy is reduced and actions are slower, but leisure has become available in abundance.

Third among the benefits of retirement is opportunity. You may not have contemplated learning a foreign language, organizing a campaign, or trying your hand at painting while work was an almost total preoccupation. Now you begin to hear of possibilities and discover skills you did not know you possessed. Your leisure can become creative.

Leisure, like work, has to be planned; otherwise time is squandered and enjoyment lost. Some people are trained planners, others need guidance. The next chapter offers a few guidelines on two basic questions: when should I start planning my retirement? and how shall I set about it?

3

Planning Your Retirement

The need to plan retirement is becoming more widely recognized. This has come as a result of the improved circumstances of the retired millions. When retirement for all but a fortunate few meant waiting to die, there was nothing to plan for or with. Men worn out with work and left in poverty had nothing better to do than nurse their exhaustion.

Today life in retirement is easier, but also more complicated. There is less extreme poverty, and there is also better health, more things to do and a longer life to enjoy doing them. But increased opportunity brings problems of choice. Retirement is a new life and you have to decide what to do with it. The over-sixties will not be content with a supine retirement.

So advice on retirement is needed more than in the past. That is, for the great majority. Some rare individuals are planners by instinct.

Some rare individuals are planners by instinct

They know what they want to do and make the transition from employment to retirement without difficulty. Books on retirement are not for them. Many other people have some rough ideas imperfectly thought out, and could benefit from guidance. Numbers of people have only the vaguest notions or none at all, and they need to be shown how and when to plan.

When should planning begin? The word implies that it comes before the event. You plan in advance. If you wait till you have retired before thinking seriously about it you are not planning but improvising. Planning must start well ahead because you are facing a situation for which you have no precedent. You are retiring for the first time in your life – and the last time too. That is why you must try to make the most of the opportunity.

There is another, equally compelling, reason for planning before retirement. You bring a fresher, younger mind to the subject. Old age is less flexible, less tolerant of change, often unfit to embark on something so complicated as a plan for living. Your plans should be tackled from strength, not weakness. Advance planning has further merits. It enables you to get used to the idea of retirement sufficiently far ahead to reduce the impact. There will be less urgency and therefore more time for thought than would be possible under the pressure of immediate need.

Planning does not come naturally to most people. In employment they do work to a plan passed down from the top. In private life they do have to make decisions, such as seeking or changing jobs, looking after and spending money, buying a car, moving house or taking out a mortgage. But retirement demands a peculiarly different decision – what to do with the rest of one's life. And it is a decision for which only the person concerned, and no one else, can be responsible.

Opinions differ about how much time to allow for retirement planning. Those who suggest six months to a year have no conception of what is involved. Five years would be barely adequate, ten years would not be too much. That is, you would have to start at fifty for retirement at sixty, and at fifty-five for sixty-five.

Those figures may surprise you. They imply that you would be thinking of retirement while you still had many years of employment and even promotion before you. But it is a sound business practice to look ahead from a peak rather than from a downward slope.

Life has other peaks than those occasioned by a career. One of the most momentous is attaining the age of fifty. It feels so much older

Half a century rings a solemn bell

than forty-nine and 364 days. Half a century rings a solemn bell. It is moreover at least two-thirds of the way through a working lifetime, and retirement begins to cast a shadow.

It is easy to find excuses for ignoring the shadow. We are all dilatory. We may genuinely intend to start thinking about retirement, but other preoccupations claim precedence, and we put off thinking again and again. After all, we say to ourselves, there is plenty of time. If we are not strict with ourselves the impulse will evaporate like New Year resolutions. Therefore we should fix a date and keep to it. And what more appropriate date than the fiftieth birthday?

It is difficult to convince people of the need for such early planning. Many treat it with derision. They have never looked at anything so far ahead. Their comment is, 'You can't avoid retirement and you can't do much about it. Let us wait till nearer the time.' Fatalism is one of the most resistant of all human attitudes.

Why should you really need so much time to plan what still seems a remote event? Because planning is not simply a matter of taking thought. It involves taking action. In less complicated times this action was called 'saving up for one's old age'. But in modern conditions there is more to save than money.

Money is still the major consideration. So much so, that a large section of this book is given over to the financial aspects of retirement. You will read about planning and handling of money for retirement in Part Three. At this stage in the discussion we need only say that what you do with your money around the age of fifty can determine how comfortably you will live from sixty-five onwards.

A LONG-RANGE PLAN

Trying to assess future conditions and needs is difficult enough in periods of political and economic stability. In these times even next year is obscure. Yet you have to peer further into the future than any business would dare to forecast. No wonder so many people shirk the attempt. But for the intelligent, responsible person there is no escape. You have to realize that, whatever the difficulties, a plan is better than no plan.

A long-range plan for a largely unpredictable future must be flexible. You will have to be prepared to modify it as your own circumstances and the economic background change. But there are a few assumptions you can safely make about your retirement, and that is where your thinking should begin.

You can assume that your total income will be lower than it is today. Pensions and savings are unlikely to equal in value what you now receive from your employment. You will live more simply, and spend less in proportion, than you do now, but in order to provide adequately for retirement you have to assume a continuing inflation. Savings and fixed incomes are more vulnerable to inflation than wages and salaries.

Your needs will be less in some directions but greater in others. In your sixties you will want comforts which younger people can forgo – for example, a house that is easier to run, warmer, safer for older and therefore more accident-prone people, and secured against the burden of rent or mortgage payments. One of the most valuable assets one might provide for old age is a house property. It would have to be suitably located for retirement. Where do you live now – in London, a suburb, an industrial city, market town, seaside resort, village? As part of your planning you will look again at your house, with the needs of the later years in mind.

It is reasonable to assume that you will be physically less strong in your sixties and after, more vulnerable to illness, more in need of protection against worry, strain and breakdown in health. Not all the disabilities of ageing can be foreseen and provided for, but some can be avoided or alleviated by planning. Fitness comes by care as well as by chance. The way you live in middle age can determine in large measure your health in old age. Changing your habits with a view to improving your health takes time. That is another reason why planning for retirement must start early. Needless to say, healthy living is worth-while for its own sake, and should start long before we detect the shadow of retirement. But at fifty we should reappraise our health as part of a project to improve our fitness and longevity.

In retirement you will have time to use or waste. What will you do with it? Which of your present activities can continue into old age? The sport and travel you enjoy may be too strenuous for you in ten to fifteen years' time. The work you are doing may be of a kind that must cease when you retire. Have you any activities that can be carried over? Or will your retirement be a vacuum? In planning it is advisable to consider what occupations and interests you have, or can acquire, that will fill the later years satisfactorily.

Part of your advance thinking might be focussed on your present job. Is there still a future in it? Have you reached a dead end at fifty or does the job still hold opportunities? If you resigned, what chance would you have of finding another job? Have you considered the possibilities of self-employment or semi-retirement with a part-time job? If you could afford to effect such a move, you could probably continue working long past the normal retirement age.

Those are just a few examples of the pre-retirement thinking on which you will base your planning. Let us make sure that we understand what is meant by thinking in this context. It does not mean sitting down with the deliberate object of thinking about retirement. That way the mind goes blank. It means getting into the habit of looking at your personality, your work, your circumstances and your environment, with eventual retirement nearer the front of your mind than it has needed to be in the past. You know how once you have become aware of a word or a fact, you find it cropping up again and again where previously it would have gone unnoticed. So it is with any subject in the forefront of your consciousness.

Thinking and planning should not be long operations. It helps to discuss some of the detail with others. Talk to retired people, find out what mistakes they made, ask if they regret not having planned well ahead, and why. Form your own opinion of how successfully they are handling their lives. Speak to your contempories among your friends and especially your colleagues whose problems may be similar to yours. Exchange of views stimulates ideas, saves the participants from thinking in a groove. If you do not learn much about what to do, you may learn what to avoid.

Above all, speak to your wife. She is more closely involved than anyone except yourself. She may have been doing her own thinking, may see things from a different angle. Joint planning is not only a matter of justice but of common sense. Though your wife does not retire when you do, and the effect on her will be less abrupt than it is upon you, her circumstances will be the reverse of yours. You will have more leisure, she will have less. She will have to adjust her routines to a new pattern to fit your new circumstances. That will be her side of the joint upheaval. The sooner you start planning your future together, the better for you both.

At the risk of being accused of self-advertisement, let us encourage you also to do some reading about retirement. There is a large literature on the subject, reflecting other people's direct experience and observation. Reading can provide practical information and general advice. But you must not expect too much from books. Your case, everyone's case, is different in important detail from anyone else's. You must grapple with those details yourself. No book is a blueprint.

A NEW MOVEMENT

A movement has been growing in the 1960s and 1970s to promote the idea of pre-retirement planning and to help people in their own plans. The leading influence is the Pre-Retirement Association of Great Britain and Northern Ireland. Its headquarters is at 19 Undine Street, Tooting, London SW17 8PP, and it has about thirty local branches throughout the country. Its membership includes businesses, professional bodies, trade unions and colleges as well as individuals.

It publishes a monthly magazine, *Choice*, which is free to members but also available from newsagents.

The PRA's function is educational. Its main work is to organize courses and seminars at the request of employers for the benefit of employees approaching retirement. The courses cover the six basic aspects of retirement: mental attitude, finance, work (paid and voluntary), health, living arrangements, and leisure activities. Within that framework the detail is tailored to the type of audience. The number of companies subscribing is increasing and so is the attendance. Wives or husbands of the participants are encouraged to attend.

If you work for an organization offering such courses you would be well advised to take part. An important feature of planning is looking out for opportunities and taking advantage of every possible facility.

One of the advantages of these courses and conferences is the opportunity they afford for discussion. You meet other people, pick up ideas, perhaps acquire new friends through recognition of common interests. You also have the benefit of individual counselling by medical, financial and vocational specialists.

If you do not live near one of the PRA branches, you can still become a member (the subscription at the time of writing is £6 a year). You will receive the magazine, and have access to advice on your personal retirement problems.

Local authorities are taking an increasing interest in retirement planning, and sponsoring courses at colleges of further education for a moderate fee. You can get particulars from your local library or adult education department.

Don't make the mistake of assuming that joining a pre-retirement seminar will be like going back to school. There are no courses of instruction or discussion anywhere that are more fully adult. There is no assembly where you will be less conspicuous. Everyone present will be in your age group and seeking the same kind of advice and information. It is all to the good that facing the problem of retirement, which till recently was solitary and secretive, should become a corporate activity. And if you think that help in planning is mainly for the ignorant, the uneducated and the humbler ranks of employee, you are equally mistaken. One of the keenest promoters of the idea of planned retirement for its members is the Institute of Directors.

When all this has been said, a reservation remains. As with books on retirement, there is a limit to the help that lecturers and seminars can be expected to provide. Experts can advise, but you have to decide and act. In the following chapter we try to devise a method of giving concrete expression to your thinking and planning.

4

A Frank Look at Yourself – Personal Audit Table

What we have done so far is to suggest ways of preparing the groundwork for your plan. You have given the subject of retirement some positive thought. You have observed and talked to other people with similar problems, and have discovered how much of your own case is common experience. You have done some reading and attended seminars and conferences which have clarified your thoughts and provided useful advice and information. Now you are ready for the plan proper.

Planning for retirement follows much the same rules as any other plan. Whatever your work has been it must have required occasional planning, if only to devise a method of tackling and completing a job. The procedure in your present plan is not basically different. First, you decide what you want to achieve: in this case a healthy, happy, active and long lived retirement. Second, you examine your present circumstances and way of life to determine how far they support or fall short of that objective. Third, you draft a course of action to make the achievement possible.

The process may be the same in principle, but the proposition is very different. In this case the workpiece is you, yourself, and the end result a pattern of living throughout all the years of your retirement. It is the most important project you have had to handle, and the most subtle. No workpiece is so variable or less easily manageable. You have to scrutinize yourself as objectively and deeply as an outside consultant would do.

Many people rarely look inward upon themselves. There may be no need. They see people, events and actions as they affect themselves rather than the other way round. They have behaved subconsciously, almost instinctively; gone after a job, made friends, got married, without deliberately thinking what kind of person they were. Indeed, they tend to be more conscious of what kind of person the other one is – a friend they can talk to and trust, a girl friend whose attraction is casual or for a lifetime, because of her qualities not theirs. If you ever had misgivings on human relations, wondered whether you were good enough for the girl (haven't we all!), you may not find an inward look at yourself too difficult.

PERSONAL AUDIT

This inward look has a practical, not an emotional purpose. In effect you are being forward-looking. Your analysis of your character, temperament and resources (mental, physical, and financial) is for action, not self-indulgence. We might call this calculated effort at self-analysis a personal audit.

It will not be easy. You have to view yourself as if you were someone else. You are closer to yourself than anyone else can be, and therefore no one can do the job for you. This self-analysis is not the same as putting yourself in the hands of a psychiatrist. It is not a medical examination but an audit, and like a business audit it must be coldly factual.

View yourself as if you were someone else

Perhaps for the first time in your life you have to enquire what kind of person you are. There is only one possible way, complete frankness. Don't try to gloss over your shortcomings or make excuses for yourself. This is not a confessional. You yourself are the sole inquisitor. No one else is asking the questions or listening to the answers. You can afford to be much less inhibited than if you had asked your friends to put you under a microscope. If you are not honest with yourself the result will be distorted. You will gain nothing but a barren self-esteem. So, let us begin.

What kind of person are you? Are you energetic or lazy, an outdoor or an indoor type, healthy, sociable, efficient, calm – or the reverse in each case? Later we shall try to tabulate various human characteristics, not in order to make ethical pronouncements but purely to see how they fit the retirement picture.

For instance, laziness may not be a disadvantage. Some people can be perfectly happy doing nothing. If they enjoy their idleness, well and good. But those who chafe at their inactivity must take themselves in hand. Boredom is a killer in retirement.

On the other hand, if you are energetic and your energies are fully exercised, you may still need to look at your activities with a critical pre-retirement eye. Will any of them last into your later years? Golf, sailing, squash may be too strenuous. In fact, you may already feel the need to ease off and find something less exacting. There is no need to be too earnest about the change or to become morbidly pre-occupied with old age. Just keep the future in mind as part of the plan.

Are you a leader or a follower? Dominant types are often domineering, and more feared than appreciated. They may be do-gooders, but their ministrations may be resented as condescending. Those qualities are generally more unpopular in women than in men. But these natural leaders are the people who get things done. They create organizations, set other people to useful work. It is these forceful men and women who manage charities and run most social activities.

Have you many interests – or few – or none? Are they a balance of indoor and outdoor, expensive and inexpensive? If so, you will have no difficulty in adjusting to the more restrictive capacities and income of retirement. If you have a single absorbing hobby, beware of letting it dominate your leisure to the exclusion of all other claims. Even admirable occupations can suffer through excess. There was a recent case of a marriage in trouble because the husband was a compulsive ntor. He spent so much time in his workshop that his wife saw even less of him in retirement than she did when he went out to a job.

Are you sociable? Do you enjoy company or is it a relief to escape? Is your wife as sociable or unsociable as you are? Being in a regular job may obscure the lack of social contacts, but when the job ceases life can become ingrown and dreary. Couples who are childless or who rarely see their children can be lonely with each other. For a retired man or woman living alone a social outlet can be a life-saver. Temperament is one of the least flexible of human attributes. A lone wolf (usually a male) is a forbidding animal. But social unease may be due to shyness or poor conversational powers, not to innate dislike of company, and there is hope in such cases. The task of building up self-confidence should start with self-examination and a frank admission of the defect.

LATENT TALENTS

We must not give the impression that a personal audit is a search for faults. The enquiry may reveal latent abilities. You may have facility in expression, a gift of humour, fluency in addressing an audience or putting over a story. Have you thought of trying to write? The experiment may not work and you should not take failure too much to heart. But it might be worth-while to make the effort, with attendance at classes if critics in your circle think you show promise. There is no easier occupation for the old than wielding a ball point pen or tapping a typewriter – physically, that is, and provided the talent is there.

The same is true of artistic talent. It is surprising how many people are good at sketching, but unaware that the talent can be developed with practice and guidance at a drawing class. Your pictures may not be saleable, but they provide an enjoyable pastime indoors and outside. A few years ago there was a vogue among American women, whose children were grown up and whose husbands were deeply immersed in business, to take lessons in drawing and painting. They were called, rather unkindly, menopause artists. No masterpiece emerged, but morale gained a big bonus. So did the impecunious professional artists who provided the tuition.

Mentally you may be as good as you have ever been: are you as fit? You do not have to be a hypochondriac to give yourself a health audit, accompanied by a medical overhaul. Normally, health is left to take care of itself. Unless there are obvious symptoms we do not give it a thought. But in planning for retirement we must take serious account of our present physical condition. It has a more powerful effect on our future than any other circumstance or characteristic.

In our grandparents' day old people used to say, lugubriously, of a person whose habits were damaging his health, 'He won't make old bones.' One of the objects of your self-examination should be to safeguard those old bones.

If it seems unrealistic in vigorous middle-life to think of old age and infirmity, one has only to remember how much ill health arises imperceptibly from habits begun in early life. Are you overweight? Some people are constitutionally heavyweights, but obesity in most cases is due to errors of diet. A later chapter will deal with dietary and other health matters in some detail. All we need say here is that if you are too fat, and self-scrutiny plus medical advice point to excesses in food and drink, start a medically approved regime without delay.

Excessive smoking has similar, and more widely publicized, long-term dangers. We are not recommending anything except self-awareness. People have a right to opt for self-indulgence whatever the consequences. But they should be aware of the consequences, not suffer injury through ignorance.

Are you efficient or slapdash, a good organizer or disorganized, patient or impatient? One of the advantages of a personal audit is that it reveals such facts about yourself through the way you handle the enquiry and document the results.

Documentation, or to say it less pompously, putting the details in orderly fashion on paper, is a useful discipline. It keeps the details before you, saves racking your memory and assists reference. You would not leave your financial accounts unrecorded. Your non-financial accounting will benefit no less from visual expression. In the pages that follow we offer a hypothetical scheme for a personal audit. You can modify it in any way you wish to suit your case. The details will differ for every individual.

Characteristics	Particulars	Comments
CATEGORY Personality and temperament		
Sociability.	Get on well with all kinds and ages of people. Good talker, good company, good neighbour. Enjoy parties. Am an exuberant, convivial type.	Sociability will be an asset in retirement, when the circle of aquaintance will need renewing. There should be no lack of company. But I must watch the conviviality. It tends to get out of control (see also *smoking* and *overweight* below)

Characteristics	Particulars	Comments
Good nature, good temper.	Easy going, sympathetic, co-operative. Work well in a team, but am not a leader. Rather easily swayed by more forceful characters.	I could do voluntary work, especially for a charity. The weakness of will is slight and may not be a serious defect in retirement, unless it results in vacillation when important decisions have to be made.
Impatience.	Too easily discouraged. Lacking in persistence.	This characteristic can become worse with age, and prove especially harmful if there is some physical incapacity. No need to be a model of efficiency, but I shall have to take initiative in organizing a satisfactory retired life and be patient enough to make the necessary adjustments.
Dilatoriness.	An associated characteristic of *good nature* and *lack of persistence* above. Intentions good, but excuses too easily found for postponing decisions and actions. Once I have taken the plunge I do generally see the job through.	Must determine to make a date with myself and stick to it. In old age time is too short for delays.
Diffidence.	A tendency to under-rate myself, which probably accounts for deficiences of will power and persistence.	Not easy to correct, despite my wife's attempts at reassurance. My *sociability* should have helped to build up my confidence. I shall think about this characteristic and decide whether it will really militate against a happy life in retirement.

CATEGORY Habits

Regular, predictable habits.	I am home-loving and apparently quite easy to live with.	My wife and I have no obvious conflicts, but as most of the things we talk about are objective, I am not sure that I know as much as I should about

Characteristics	Particulars	Comments
		what she thinks. Must ask her if I have any irritating quirks which will drive her mad when I am home for most of the day.
Rather untidy; tend to mislay things.	A habit due to hurry. It started when I was afraid to be late for school and has continued as part of the rush to work.	I am orderly enough in my work, so it should not be difficult to be less careless at home. My wife has been tolerant, but this may actually be one of the quirks that annoys her.
Injudicious smoking, drinking and eating.	I am not an addict, but I have a tendency to excess, especially on social occasions. I suppose I would be called a good trencherman, and can hold my liquor fairly well.	Apart from the health factor, which is the most important of all, I may not be able to afford so much indulgence when I retire. Will try to limit the drinks and curb greed. Also experiment to see whether it will be easier to reduce my smoking or cut it out altogether.

CATEGORY Health and physical condition

Characteristics	Particulars	Comments
Muscular and energetic.	I enjoy physical exertion, take plenty of exercise, do not tire quickly; but suspect that I do not always know when I've had enough.	Exercise is good at any age but I am inclined to overdo it. Nothing wrong with the heart, but breath not what it was, and friends and doctor advise a judicious slowing down. Am in no danger of becoming a hypochondriac.
Getting overweight.	I have a healthy digestion and enjoy rich food, therefore in spite of exercise a paunch is beginning to show.	Time to start dieting. Must ask the doctor for a not-too-austere chart. Have noticed that the fittest old men I know are generally the thin ones.
Slightly chesty.	I have few of the aches and pains of middle age, no rheumatism or arthritis, but get a cough and slight wheeziness lasting a few weeks in mid-autumn.	A warning to cut smoking. Must avoid becoming bronchial in the later years.

Characteristics	Particulars	Comments
CATEGORY Interests		
Sport.	Tennis, golf, swimming, watching football.	Tennis may be too strenuous in ten or fifteen years' time and I ought to find an alternative that will last almost indefinitely. Bowls doesn't appeal much but it might be advisable to try it.
Games.	Darts, billiards and most table games from Scrabble to snakes and ladders.	Darts and billiards are harmless enough, but they take place in the pub and club with too much alcoholic accompaniment. If I can control the intake both games should remain an active interest as long as hand and eye keep true.
Walking.	I am an all-weather walker.	This, and the following, are life-long interests.
Gardening.	I provide the labour and my wife the green fingers.	Walking and gardening will have to be less strenuous as I grow older.
Light reading. Television and radio. Theatre.	I am not a TV addict, but am interested in sports, news and political programmes.	Television and reading will claim more attention as reduced energy and finances cut down visits to the theatre.
Collecting.	Walking sticks and old gramophone records.	I shall have more time in retirement to nose round the junk markets and, if finance permits, add to my collections.
CATEGORY Accomplishments.		
Manual skill.	I am mechanically minded, able to handle many of the odd jobs in a house without having to hire help. I am a competent driver, understand cars and like tinkering with them.	For health reasons at least, I shall continue to see that I get enough walking. I know too many men who don't go a hundred yards without the car.

Characteristics	Particulars	Comments
Draughtsmanship	My job has involved engineering drawing.	I might try my hand at other kinds of drawing. It is a pleasant hobby and has the merit of costing very little.
Photography.	Have done some semi-professional photographing of machinery, but am a reasonably good amateur on scenes and portraits.	Colour photography can be rather expensive but I need not be too ambitious. Might do my own black and white developing and printing. Perhaps fix up a dark room in a corner of the garage or the garden shed.

CATEGORY Living conditions.

Three-bedroom semi-detached house with garden in a London suburb.	Two more years of the mortgage to go.	Three bedrooms are more than two people need. Must look into the economics of selling the house and buying a bungalow. If we keep the house we shall have to think of labour-saving changes such as built-in wardrobes and paving part of the garden. (House and location are the most problematic items in the audit, and it may take a few years to reach the most sensible decisions on them.)

As you see, the audit is broadly classified into six divisions which correspond to the six main topics of any pre-retirement study. Those are standard for all cases. The variables are in the detail, the comments and the decision. The significant fact about a personal audit is that it is personal.

We said that the 'auditor' would have to be frank about his character and personality. But frankness works two ways. You have to list your virtues as well as your faults and you must not be coy about doing so. The audit is not an exercise in self-praise or in self-abasement. It is a self-assessment with the best motives: to use whatever good qualities you may have and to look critically at those which are not so good, so that you will be able to make the best of your retirement.

Not everyone is capable of viewing himself in quite so hard a light as our specimen planner. We have chosen an ideal (or perhaps an extreme) case of self-awareness. Actual planners will handle the task as well as their vision permits.

In any case your audit will not be a complete self-analysis. It will be severely practical and relevant only to your retirement. Your intellect, your beliefs and your morals may be irrelevant in this context. For instance, if you eat, drink or smoke to excess you may or may not feel shame, make vows and do penance. What you have to do is relate these excesses to your present health and to your longevity and means in a retired old age.

The specimen audit shown is very much abridged. You may want to amplify it in all directions, list more habits and interests, dig deeper into matters of health, greatly enlarge the pros and cons of changing house and habitat. You will adapt it as you think fit.

You will learn a good deal about yourself in the course of making this pen portrait. It may be a chastening experience, but not, we hope, a depressing one. The audit cannot be exhaustive. What you get out of it will be limited by your understanding of your own nature and of human nature in general. Some questions are difficult to answer because they involve comparisons with the average, and only a psychologist could tackle them with any precision (and even he could give a wrong answer). In addition to elements in character and temperament that elude us through ignorance, there are probably some that even the frankest of us are unwilling to admit to ourselves. But there will be enough for our purpose.

One of the advantages of a plan on paper, as we have suggested, is that it facilitates cross-referencing. You can see how characteristics build up into a life-style and reinforce each other beneficially or otherwise. For instance, you can see the influence of social qualities and sport upon health, and the effect of temperament and habit upon capability and fulfilment.

Having got your audit, use it. It is a programme for action. It shows gaps in your circumstances to be filled or circumvented, inadequacies in yourself to be corrected or lived with, possibilities to be studied and followed up. Don't put it aside and pat yourself on the back for something attempted, something done. It is not an end in itself but a means to an end. Bring it up to date, have second thoughts, improve the plan and the prescriptions for action as you go along.

Like your initial thinking, the written plan might benefit from other people's suggestions and advice. There is a difficulty here. The more intimate and revealing the document is, the more reluctant you will

Show your personal audit to your wife

be to show it to others. You might be glad of the opinion of one or two old friends. You will certainly show it to your wife, who took part in the thinking that led up to it. Ask her to be as frank with you as you have been with yourself. This is no occasion for protecting the ego, but for realism. She may actually find some of your strictures on yourself too harsh.

There is a glaring but deliberate omission from the audit. It is as vital as health but in many ways more complex and perhaps more technical. It is the financial aspect of retirement – how to look after your money, invest wisely, budget carefully, and make sure that you can afford most of the things you want to do. Money must have a separate audit. It occupies the whole of Part Three.

PART TWO

Living in Retirement

5
Mind Over Matter

We have looked at many factors that affect our chances of happiness in retirement. All are important, but two are vital. These are money and health bracketed equally at the head of the list. We must have enough money to live on and good enough health to make living worth-while. Both of these resources can be enlarged and strengthened by wise management as we shall try to show in detail later. Let us look first at health.

In some respects money and health support (or frustrate) each other. Good health is an economy and ill health is expensive in spite of the concessions that social security makes to the aged sick. Subscribers to BUPA and similar schemes outside the National Health Service sometimes find that money can buy health. What it will not buy, of course, is a cure for ageing. Yet some people think against all logic that it should.

Resistance to the fact of growing old is natural. Ageing is a succession of deprivations. Energies diminish, activities are restricted, pleasures recede, and the future shrinks alarmingly. A negative attitude shows old age to be a calamity. 'Sans teeth, sans eyes, sans taste, sans everything', as Shakespeare's greatest pessimist was made to say.

But there is a positive point of view which brings some light into the gloom. Old age is evidence of survival. Those who grow old have escaped dying young. They have lived long enough to retire. Ageing is therefore inseparable from retirement. Young people don't retire. A model may announce her retirement in her late twenties to open a boutique. A boxer may realize he is too old for the ring at thirty-odd and put his savings into a pub. That is not retirement but reorientation.

True retirement means that the capacity for a complete occupational change of direction has gone.

Very few people retire in middle age, except for reasons of health or infirmity. Even those who can easily afford to retire prefer to go on working. The newly retired at sixty-plus may also be capable of continuing in a full-time job. They are far from being decrepit. But, as they admit ruefully and irrelevantly, 'they are not as young as they were.' If they are inclined to forget that fact employers will remind them.

IMPORTANCE OF MORALE

How soon and how successfully we come to terms with old age depends on morale. And morale can have a profound effect on health. Low morale is not strictly speaking a mental aberration. It is not a disease or a direct cause of disease. But it causes depression and apathy, which reduce vitality, debilitate the body, and make it vulnerable to disease. We show the effect in our faces and behaviour. We look the way we feel.

There are social repercussions. People tend to avoid those who make them miserable. Even those who respond sympathetically to genuine illness and disability are repelled by pessimism. There is a limit to the patience with which they will listen to a self-pitying monologue.

One of the saddest features of resistance to the facts of ageing is that it worsens the condition. Excessive worry about growing old makes you grow old more quickly. Cheerful elders look and feel younger than their dismal contemporaries.

It is not easy to overcome the obsession with the depredations of age. Appeals to reason make little headway against the congenital stronghold of temperament. It has to be breached from within by a process of do-it-yourself sanity. When Thomas Carlyle was told that Margaret Fuller, a nineteenth-century American author, had declared, 'I accept the universe,' he growled, 'By Gad, she'd better.' And by Gad we'd all better accept the facts of ageing.

The older we get the more difficult it is to modify temperament and change the notions it generates. If the task is left till retirement it may be impossible. Age hardens the mind as well as the arteries. But if you have done your pre-retirement audit, many retirement difficulties will have been foreseen and averted. The audit has not been a once-for-all exercise but a continuing plan of action. You have checked up on it, recorded achievements, changes of mind, negligence and failure.

Let us look at our hypothetical case again and see how it prevented some of the worst effects of unplanned retirement.

The very fact of having faced retirement with an early plan gave him a hedge against shock and depression. He was familiar with many of the problems even if he had not solved them. He did not have to start on or near retirement-day wondering what he was going to do. He had done something already and had a pretty good idea of what remained to be done. The plan had given him ten years' start over the majority of people approaching retirement.

In spite of a lively performance when in company, and an apparently buoyant outlook on life, he had some inhibitions. He was easily discouraged, tended to under-rate his qualities. If not corrected these characteristics could have led to impatience with the disabilities of ageing and ultimately to demoralization. But there was a saving grace. His social success did not diminish with the years. He was sought after for his gift of anecdote and repartee. He was popular with young people. Evidently he was not a candidate for the back seats. Morale remained high.

Under gentle prodding from his wife, and in spite of many lapses, he did something about his untidiness. He had seen a retired relative develop slack habits and took the warning. He tried to remember to put his clothes neatly away, made less litter for others to clear. Without becoming fussy he gradually acquired more orderly habits. Domestic relations benefited and so did his self-respect.

He took to heart what the personal audit had taught him about health. Overweight was the big worry. Apart from the risk to health, it aged him. He knew that fat people looked older than thin people of the same age. Despite spells of backsliding he reduced the paunch with diet and exercise. He was less puffy after games, and that confirmed that he was on the right lines.

There was a financial bonus. The suits that had been getting tight fitted better, and replacements could wait. There was a bonus of another kind. His wife was anxious to avoid a weight problem and went on the same diet. While it is not true that two can diet as cheaply as one, catering is easier and perhaps a little cheaper with one lot of cooking instead of two.

Drinking and smoking proved more difficult to control than eating. But a drinking bout sometimes had its moment of revelation. There was a brief interval between ordinary enjoyment and not giving a damn, when he was aware that he was being rather silly, and that some of the laughter was not so much with him as against him. Recognizing when enough is enough is the beginning of wisdom.

Other habits needed little or no change. Our planner's enjoyment of walking became almost a ritual daily airing in retirement. He added bowls to his list of sports, kept up his swimming, played a bit of golf but dropped tennis. He started helping in a senior citizens' club and the sense that he was on the giving instead of the receiving end was quite a morale-booster.

His wife was encouraging. She shared many of his interests and helped to keep the plan alive. They talked frankly about what age does to the face, the figure, the vitality and the mind, and decided that they were not doing badly for their years. They also agreed that they could do even better (he especially) with attention to dress and grooming. She took charge of keeping up appearances and improving the image.

They did not sell their house before retirement, but left that decision open. There would be time enough when they could no longer cope with the stairs. But they provided against the time when the garden would be beyond their strength by selling half of it to younger neighbours who wanted to enlarge theirs. Part of the money was used to pave the front garden and buy tubs. There was enough garden left for pleasure, but not so much to tie them down.

They took stock of their capital, income and expenditure, much on the lines recommended in Part Three. They planned for the years when there might be no earnings, and when income would be more desirable than growth as a return on investment. They scrutinized their living costs for possibilities of economy.

MYTHS ABOUT RETIREMENT

Among the subjects they had to clear up in their minds were the myths that have arisen about retirement. One of them is that you age more quickly after retirement. It need not be so. As we have seen, the mind plays a large part in making people older or keeping them younger than their years. Illness, shock and disaster can put years on us, but that can happen at any age. If we persuade ourselves that retirement is a tragedy, ageing will accelerate, but it will be the thought and not the circumstance that speeds the process.

No less enervating is the thought that retirement is a dead end. You have been swept out of the main stream of life, into a backwater where there is nothing but stagnation. Again, this need not come true. Retirement can be a turning instead of an end. The pre-retirement plan should not be regarded as a formula for life in the years ahead. You can explore new ideas and acquire new interests which you could not have foreseen years ago at the planning stage. Retirement can be more creative than the working years because you have so much more free time.

Yet another myth is that you are more dependent in retirement. You may depend to some extent on the national retirement pension and possibly supplementary benefits, but these represent the maturing of a partly contributory insurance. You will be dependent in other ways in sickness or extreme age, but retirement will not be the cause. In general we are more independent in retirement, freed from the obligations to an employer, a timetable and a living. We can live our lives very much as we wish.

If all this sounds like a moral tale followed by a sermon we offer no apologies. Morale is to the mind what vitamins are to the body. In the old it can be a matter of life or death. It keeps you forward-looking, convinces you that you have a future. As indeed you have. At sixty-five, barring accidents and unavoidable illness, you can have twenty or more years of worth-while life.

Those years will be worth-while if we make them so. Early planning helps, but the fulfilment has to await retirement. Morale is a state of mind but it depends for its sustenance on the way we live.

Our hypothetical planner was not typical – there is no such thing. There are so many variables in human character, background, tastes, education, and financial circumstances, and so many possible combinations, that no example will fit any individual case. But if you do not see yourself in the detail, you will probably find a general affinity. Most of the factors that assist morale apply to us all.

We should eliminate from the list those that bestow a false and temporary morale. Alcohol springs immediately to mind. Drink is one of the most abused (in both senses of the term) of human pleasures. It is not abused in either sense by epicures. Those who misuse it to drown their miseries usually dredge up something which is neither pleasurable nor therapeutic. There is no medicine to restore morale.

What is true of alcohol is no less true of tranquillizers. These have their place in medical practice and have proved valuable in treating depressive conditions. They were not intended for indiscriminate use. They were certainly not intended as aids to coping with the normal stresses of life. People are taking them to escape from boredom or from taking responsibility. They do not cure our troubles: they help us to ignore them. They can become an addiction, destroying instead of enhancing morale. One of the most alarming aspects of this form of indulgence is that it is so widespread. It is coming to be regarded as normal. When you are asked, 'What pills are you taking?' and you say, 'None at all', you are either disbelieved or labelled eccentric.

The reason for escapism through drugs is clear enough. Strong characters face the situation, weak characters seek oblivion. Between the two are the majority of people, who are not beyond reason and need advice in varying degrees. Once they have accepted the fact that morale comes from within and not from the chemist they will be open to rational suggestions.

Of course, taking oneself in hand is easier for some people than for others, and easier in some directions than in others. Our retirement planner had no difficulty in the social sphere. He was a born mixer. Others are not so fortunately endowed. They are reserved, self-conscious and, in extreme cases, friendless. For them it is an effort to make human contacts.

On the other hand, our extroverted friend found social ease beset with temptations. It was an effort to cut down food, drink and smokes, embarrassing to refuse the appeal, 'Come on, just one more', or the more insidious 'It's not like you to quit.' Every person has to make his own more or less painful adjustments.

Even sociable types have to give some attention to their social life in retirement. The circle of acquaintance shrinks when you retire. You are separated from colleagues whom you used to see every working day. Unless you made some lasting friendships on the job you will have to rely on old friends and relatives. Most of your old friends will be about your own age and you may outlive some of them. Life will be quieter and slower as you grow older.

You may not mind slowing down. Energy diminishes and so does spending power. You will in any case do less entertaining. But don't let your social activities run down through neglect. Choose a few activities (through clubs, societies and avocations) which will put you in touch with new faces and minds. Meeting people is stimulating even if you never get on visiting terms.

Getting acquainted is easier in large families than in small, easier for couples than for those whom sociologists so bleakly call 'single-tons'. If one has brothers, sisters and in-laws there will be a social pool out of which new friendships may arise. Husband and wife support each other socially and may each make new friends. But the widowed and the unmarried of both sexes may be very lonely and neglected in retirement.

The obvious source of companionship is among those in similar circumstances. Anyone who is diffident about making an approach should bear in mind that the other person may be equally so. What looks at first like unapproachability may be nothing more forbidding than shyness and fear of a rebuff. Lone wolves who enjoy their immunity from contact are fortunately very rare. One has to conquer timidity and risk a brush-off. It is a remote risk. A warm welcome is much more likely.

FIT FOR YOUNGER COMPANY

It is very important for elderly people to move in mixed company. Naturally, they have more sympathy with those of their own age group. But in an exclusively ageing circle all become more deeply ingrown and less fit for younger company. Small worlds of any kind tend to become inhuman. A closed circle of accountants, anglers, economists or footballers can be even more limiting than a miscellaneous bunch of elders.

It is a fallacy to suppose that old and young do not mix. Young people are not hostile to the old. They are, however, wary. They are not sure how they will be received. If there is no possibility of contact, the old are usually at fault. It is for them to make the first approach. Though less flexible than the young, their long experience should have given them enough poise to bridge the gap. If they like young people all obstacles will disappear.

There's the rub. You have to like younger people or at least try to understand them. Many of their values will differ from yours. They may lack some of the graces you were brought up with, but will be less inhibited in thought and expression. They believe they are emancipated and will not welcome any suggestion that in fact they conform to the standards of their set as you did to yours. They don't expect you to agree with their views – they would rather you didn't – but you should at least take them seriously.

Don't make the mistake of accepting their tastes and ideas whole-heartedly. They will see through the deception. You don't have to pretend that you enjoy their music, nor should you decry it. Between the old and the young, as was said in another connection, vive la différence. Fraternizing is a form of condescension and will be resented.

No less galling than condescension is an air of superiority. Some things may have been better in our young days, but we cannot expect today's young people to believe it. They have no direct means of comparison. Indeed they may be right in believing that some things have improved. Mixing with younger people can be an education for the old, and vice versa.

Younger people can be exasperating. They have their own forms of condescension. Elderly ladies bridle to hear themselves called 'old dears'. (There are less polite epithets for old gentlemen which actually give less offence.) It is wiser to ignore the insult. An angry old man (or woman) is a more deplorable sight than an 'angry young man'.

Age is a state of mind as well as of body. Each can age at different rates. It is the aged mind, not the lined face, that young people find forbidding. We knew a bright and brisk gentleman in his late eighties who said he had chosen one holiday hotel in preference to another because he 'didn't want to be stuck with a lot of old people'.

It is well known that the mind can remain youthful longer than the body. We should therefore avoid exaggerating its rejuvenating influence on the body. Physical deterioration may be the result of ill health or it may be constitutional. Some people have always seemed older than their years. It is not helpful in such cases to quote shining examples. An orchestra conductor who is still working and travelling around the world in his eighties offers no encouragement to lesser men and women. But Renoir, who had a brush tied to his paralysed hand and continued painting, does present a mind-over-matter lesson for non-geniuses.

The mind responds to stimulus. Like the muscles it remains flexible through use. If you have lots of interests you will leave few loop-holes for brooding on the less cheerful aspects of ageing. Interests are progressive. You look forward to the next phase or development, and the subject expands as your interest deepens.

The choice of subjects is vast and varied. We shall deal with them in another chapter. There is something for every kind of mind: intellectual, artistic, technical, administrative, sporting, charitable. They can be physically active or sedentary according to your energies and inclinations. Some of them will stretch your mind, others just entertain. You can be giver or receiver, or both. These interests are capable of almost any combination that your physical, mental and financial capacities will tolerate.

Nobody is without interests, but they can be too few, too rarely available, or too expensive to be adequate for people with abundant leisure. A passion for the ballet or for a seasonal interest such as cricket should be part of a balanced mental diet. Artistic and intellectual pursuits are all the better for some accompanying roughage. Etching and tiddlywinks are not incompatible.

DEVELOPING INTERESTS

If your interests are limited in number and scope, how do you acquire others? There is no simple or completely satisfactory answer. You can't buy or force an interest. It has to find a responsive chord inside you or it will be a bore. On the other hand it is useless to hope that something will turn up. The best way is by trial and error. You may see something on television or read about it in the newspaper and feel a mild interest. That is your clue to seek more information. For instance, you may be a casual amateur photographer, snapping your family and friends and holiday scenes, but little else. Then after seeing an illustrated magazine feature on church architecture you photograph a few churches in your neighbourhood. That strikes a spark. You borrow books on nineteenth-century church architecture from the library, look further afield for subjects, and start your own photograph album. In exploring for churches you may find other things to interest you – epitaphs, wrought-iron-work, birds and beasts of the hedges.

Another example. You are handy in the house and a careful worker. When a cup handle breaks off you can stick it neatly back. You can do a competent repair on damaged woodwork. But you had not thought of trying renovation till you noticed a list of handicraft courses in a college prospectus. With practical guidance you take up china repair and produce some creditable specimens out of imperfect ornaments picked up in junk shops.

A useful way to enlarge your own range of interests is to notice what other people do. They will be flattered by your attention and willing to share experience.

As you have gathered, nothing happens unless you open your mind so that ideas can enter. You have to be aware of a need and look out for opportunities to satisfy it. And one possibility can lead to others by a kind of chain reaction. There is rarely a good excuse for failing to find enough occupation in retirement.

The image you present can make all the difference between success and failure in social contacts. It is in itself an important influence on morale. We have referred briefly to the danger of slack habits – slopping around in dressing gown and slippers long after breakfast,

Notice what other people do

uncombed and unshaven, just because the compulsion of employment no longer exists. There is more to it than that. The careless habit can become a life-style. You may cease to care how you look.

Obviously there is no need for formal dress in retirement. If your job required you to wear a suit, it is a relief and also an economy to concentrate on casuals. But the baggy trousers and out-at-elbows sweater which will do for the garden or odd jobs are not suitable for regular wear. Let the neighbours see that inside the casual labourer there is a gent who has no difficulty in getting out.

In the heyday of imperialism there was a joke about British empire-builders who insisted upon dressing for dinner in the jungle. Behind the exaggeration there was a grain of good sense. There are circumstances in which standards have to be protected against decay by a deliberate effort. We must be as civilized in retirement as we were in employment.

Grooming for the male adds little to the budget. A clean shave is as simple as a rough one. Bristles left around the Adam's apple are pathetically unsightly in an old man. Hair should be kept well trimmed. Straggling locks have become acceptable in the young, but in the old they are slovenly. So is dandruff. If there is no cure, frequent washing of the head and brushing of the coat collar should be good enough. Greying and balding are so common from middle age onwards that most of us don't worry; but if you think a wig will make you look younger and smarter, go ahead.

A lined face is ageing, and some skins are naturally more wrinkle-prone than others. The habit of grimacing adds unnecessarily to the creases. If you frown, it may be because you need a change of glasses, and more than your appearance will benefit.

A good appearance is even more important for women. It is also more expensive. Even the reduced price for a perm offered by hair-dressers on certain days to senior citizens can be a burden, but it is worth-while. The contrast between 'a nice old lady' and 'a poor old thing' is not necessarily a matter of money. Good taste in dress need not be more costly than bad. Fashion is a tyrant at all ages, but women can find expedients (ringing the changes with separates, even judicious swapping with other women) to look good without going broke.

Old age is harder in this respect on women than on men. It does more violence to face and figures and therefore to morale. Volumes of advice have been written on the subject. It is one of the repetitive regulars in women's magazines, which usually report accurately and helpfully. As with men, the signs of ageing can be delayed or masked by common-sense living and behaviour. There are a few exceptions. Since women worry more about appearance they tend towards excess in corrective measures. A common fault is to overdo the slimming. The skin is less elastic in age, and does not recover completely after stretching through overweight. Elderly women who are not naturally thin must be reconciled to rather more weight than they would like.

A second example is make-up. It can work wonders or horrors. A woman in her sixties who makes up as if she were in her thirties merely magnifies the ravages of age. Most women know this, and most of those who don't are unteachable. The main risk with women, as with men, is that apathy may take over in the seventies, a belief that it doesn't matter any more. That is where morale breaks down and despair sets in. And that is where some of the reminders in this chapter may be useful in helping to prolong good habits and good sense.

6

Eat, Drink and be ... Sensible

A healthy mind in a healthy body is a centuries-old prescription for a balanced human condition. We have looked into health of mind and spirit and its influence upon the body. Let us now consider physical well-being in itself.

It is largely a product of our way of life. We can choose to live sensibly or foolishly within our means. The qualification is important, and is implicit in every chapter of this book. If we cannot afford many of the things that promote healthy and comfortable living we have to accept the limitation. But observation of those who are better off, and a reading of the newspapers, provides evidence that the means and the good sense do not always coincide. It is easier for the rich to indulge intemperate impulses.

Food and drink come high in the list of temptations to error and excess. The simple facts are that over-indulgence in food and alcohol generally results in overweight. Obesity puts a strain on the heart. Fat people are more prone to coronaries and their expectation of life is lower than for people of normal weight. Some insurance companies make this very plain to applicants for life policies.

To keep one's weight down is not specially prescribed for pre-retirement planning. It is important at any age. Indeed, wrong feeding is becoming endemic in Britain. You have only to notice a troop of schoolchildren. Most of them are bigger and fitter, because they are better fed, than our generation was. But the proportion of fat children is alarming.

Affluence plus ignorance is manifested in the same way among adults. But especially among the old. In a bus load of concession pass-holders a thin person is engulfed. You marvel that the majority have survived so far. Overweight among the old must be mainly due to neglect in earlier years.

Mainly – but not entirely. Elderly people, especially in retirement, lead less active, more sedentary lives, and need less food than they did even in middle age. But there is an element of habit in eating. Many people continue to eat as much as before, when they need less, and the excess turns to fat.

Let us be clear about dieting. It does not always mean eating less. You can lose weight by starving, as the pitiful victims of Nazism did in Belsen. The purpose of slimming is to correct an imbalance. Intelligent feeding, not starvation, is the key.

Intelligent feeding requires a little knowledge about the nature of food and how it affects our bodies. That knowledge is not highly scientific or difficult to acquire. Any general encyclopedia contains the basic details. Newspapers and popular magazines repeat them in innumerable articles. Every pre-retirement course includes instruction on diet. No one who can read should have difficulty in finding the facts. We suspect that more people know the facts than are willing to apply them, but that is another story.

There are three broad categories of food: protein, carbohydrates and fats. The elementary definition of their function is that proteins make good the wear and tear on the body's tissues, while carbohydrates and fats provide heat and energy. The protein foods are mainly meat, fish, eggs, cheese and milk; the carbohydrates are cereals, starchy vegetables and sugar; the fats are animal and vegetable fats, butter and margarine. But these are not closed categories. Lean meat contains enough fat for normal needs. Bread contains protein as well as carbohydrate. Starches and sugars in excess of energy needs produce fat in the body.

It is because of this overlapping of categories that we need not measure our meals as if they were medicines or ingredients in a recipe. People in normal health who are neither fat nor emaciated need not think anxiously about their diet. They are getting an adequate balance of basic foods and of the necessary supplementary and trace elements.

These additional elements are vitamins, minerals and roughage. They are more noticeable by their absence than their presence. If your diet includes fresh fruit and vegetables you can – other conditions being equal – ignore the warnings and calculations of dieticians. These will be more suitable for faddists and sufferers from defects of diet.

Even faddists may be getting a perfectly satisfactory diet. A vegetarian diet can be medically sound. So can 'health' foods. Preoccupation with diet when there is no pressing medical need may amuse or repel the more carefree majority, but if it works for the devotees it should not be condemned. What you fancy, within reason, whether free-range chicken or nut cutlets, will do you good. It takes a large variety of habits to make a normal community.

THE WEIGHT PROBLEM

So much for the norm. But the overweight are abnormal. They may not be gross enough for adverse comment, but they are at risk. Dieting for them is not a fad but a life-saver. It will not mean going hungry, though their favourite foods will be sadly missed for a time. They will reduce their intake of bread, potatoes, fried foods, fats and rich and starchy puddings, reduce the three spoons of sugar in their tea to one (or preferably none), eat salads and green vegetables. Alcoholic drinks, especially beer, will be reduced. Cakes, biscuits, chocolates and all sugary snacks, solid or liquid, are taboo.

A reducing diet is measured in terms of the calorific values of foodstuffs. Calories are units of heat or energy, or in other words a measure of the conversion value of food into fuel. A hard-working human engine, as in an athlete or a roustabout on an oil rig, needs more fuel than an engine that ticks over gently, as in a desk-bound or retired person. If more calories are taken in than the engine needs to burn, the surplus is stored in the body as fat. Dieticians have calculated the required daily intake of calories for people of various weights and levels of physical activity. In general, the old need fewer calories than the young because they are less active and consume less energy.

Calories have no bearing on mental energy. The mind is sustained and activated by more intangible fuels. That is why sedentary workers, however intellectually exacting their work may be, do not need a high-calorie diet. It must be remembered though that the condition of the body affects the functioning of the brain as it does that of the other organs.

It is possible, with minimal arithmetic, kitchen scales, and the help of food value tables in a book on diet borrowed from your public library, to calculate a slimming diet for yourself. But it is not a good idea. Man (and woman) cannot live by calories alone. A diet can be calorie perfect and still be deficient. The body is a complex organism that becomes extra vulnerable and has special needs as it ages.

Counting calories

Excessive weight is a condition of ill health. For that reason it would not be helpful to give details here about desirable body weights and calorie requirements. Human beings, whether working or retired, male or female, young, middle-aged or old, small-framed or big-boned, short or tall or somewhere in between, are still varied in too many ways for unskilled prescription to be either useful or safe. Unfortunately, too few doctors understand dieting. There are, however, many reliable and helpful books on slimming.

Why some people can eat whatever they like and remain slim, while others have to weigh up every ounce of indulgence in fattening food, is not fully understood. You may not know the reason but you can't ignore the fact with impunity. The metabolism is not fooled. You can tell yourself that 'just this once won't make any difference', and if it is just this once it won't. But if you say it repeatedly and believe it each time you will pay the price. You have to choose between a possibly shorter chubby life and a longer one of dietetic restraint.

If you are strong-minded, it need not be too austere. You can relax on fairly rare occasions (Christmas or a wedding) without suffering a setback. But if you can't trust yourself, keep strictly to the diet. You will be surprised how one can get used to a diet and even like it.

A sad fact about special diets is the cost. Carbohydrates are filling and comparatively cheap. The very poor still tend to fill up on bread and potatoes, and may suffer from malnutrition and overweight at the same time. Weight for weight, proteins are the most expensive foods, but they are satisfying in comparatively small quantities. Salads are fairly expensive and bulky but not sustaining: their function is to supply roughage for healthy bowel action and also essential vitamins and minerals. If you are overweight you will have to regard the special diet as a form of medical treatment.

You may not know the ideal weight for your age, size and occupation, but you will know if you are getting too fat. If you have more flab than muscle and a growing paunch, if your trousers (or skirts) are less comfortable round the middle and your belt has to be eased a notch, you need advice. Weigh yourself once a month. Ignore an increase of a few pounds if it goes no further, but a consistent increase should be taken seriously. If you are thin and healthy, be thankful. But if you are losing weight ask your doctor why.

If you are fit and have no weight problems, you will want to remain so. Therefore there are still some dietary rules to observe. They depend upon common knowledge and common sense. Maintenance is not a skilled job.

How much should you eat? The answer is, not more than you need. One substantial meal a day, and two much lighter ones, should be enough for the elderly, and for most of their juniors too. Digestion, like other bodily functions, becomes less efficient as we get older.

It doesn't matter when you have your main meal. You may like a traditional English or else a Continental breakfast, a three-course meal at midday and a light evening meal, or you may prefer some other combination. But you should balance your intake so that moderation remains the rule.

You will have more home-cooking in retirement. The food will probably be better cooked and tastier than what you ate in a canteen or restaurant. You will be tempted to do it over-full justice. Self-discipline is an important additive.

Having established a regimen, don't defeat it by nibbling between meals, except under doctor's orders. If you have a troublesome duodenum, you may be told to eat little and often; but you will have to obey both halves of that prescription. The total intake will still be moderate.

What should you eat? As with quantity, so with the kind of food. You should aim at a balanced diet. It will consist of the essentials we have mentioned – protein and carbohydrate, a certain amount of roughage, and additional foods which will make good any lack of vitamins and minerals in the main ingredients. These will not all be included in every meal, but as far as possible in each day's total.

Balance does not exclude variety. In fact a varied diet is necessary to keep up your interest in food. You will ring the changes on red meat, poultry, prepared meats and fish to suit your tastes and pocket. You will include greens as well as potatoes, root crops and the pulses (beans, peas and lentils) in your rota of vegetables. Muesli is a good and very palatable source of fibre.

In a varied diet of that kind you will get all the fat you need. Only if you are specially fond of fat will you have to watch the kind and quantity consumed. Fats not only have a very high calorific value but, in the opinion of many medical authorities, animal fats ('saturated fats' in scientific language) are also a cause of arterial and cardiac disorders. If you must have occasional fried foods use vegetable fats such as olive oil and corn oil instead of butter and lard.

Sugar is one of the concealed indulgencies. Addicts forgo chocolates, but eat quantities of cake and tinned fruit; they use chemical sweetners in their tea, but pile sugar on porridge and cornflakes – and they think they are slimming. The British are the biggest sugar consumers in the world. It damages their teeth in childhood, increases weight and acidity at all ages, and contributes nothing of value to nutrition.

Food processing has increased the sugar in food but reduced the roughage. As a result our diet is too bland. Roughage provides the undigested bulk which the bowels need for regular and easy elimination. That bulk is the fibrous element in salads, green vegetables, the pulses, citrus fruits, muesli, and the bran in wholemeal bread. If you were forced to eat cabbage in childhood and have hated it ever since, remember that it really is 'good for you' as your parents said so persistently. And if you prefer white bread for toasting, add some bran to your cereal in compensation.

We have said nothing about liquids. Tea is the great standby, especially with women. Plain water is what nature intended, though one must admit that beer, and cider (dry for preference) are more palatable, and more wholesome than most soft drinks. Milk is too substantial to be treated as a thirst-quencher. Some elderly people have too little liquid, perhaps because they are worried over a bladder weakness, and become dehydrated without knowing it. Diet manuals tell us how many pints a day we need, but only eccentrics or invalids would bother to measure. The equivalent of eight or nine teacups a day, on average, should be enough for ordinary needs.

Should we add vitamins to our diet? It is rare for people in Britain to suffer from vitamin deficiency. A balanced diet will provide all we need. There is vitamin A in liver, carrots and tomatoes, vitamin B in meat (especially liver), brown bread, green vegetables and peanuts, vitamin C in citrus fruits and most fresh vegetables, and vitamin D in milk, butter and margarine. We gain nothing by taking extra vitamins unless medically specified. The surplus does not make us super-fit; it is excreted or may do harm.

The very old may have a deficient diet through poverty, ignorance or sheer neglect. Some have a poor appetite and do not eat enough. Some have badly fitting false teeth and avoid foods that need chewing. Theirs is a partly social, partly medical problem. Self-neglect is not exclusive to the senile. People who should know better eat unwisely, living out of tins or packets, eating at irregular times because their time is their own, running around with a sandwich instead of sitting down to a meal. Retired people living alone are the chief offenders — perhaps we ought to say sufferers. Retirement should make no difference to your pattern of eating. It *should* make a beneficial difference to your meal-time habits. Since there is no need to hurry, eat slowly and enjoy your food.

DRINK AND SMOKING

We have spoken with approval of alcohol as a food accompaniment. But alcohol, as we know, is a wayward companion. In excess it depresses the appetite instead of stimulating it. Even those who hold their liquor well may suffer the effects. Though heavy drinkers eat less they don't get thinner. Alcoholic drinks increase one's weight without improving nutrition. There are sound medical reasons for moderation in drinking.

An ageing digestive system cannot take the punishment of hard liquor on an empty stomach. Beer will be less damaging than spirits so long as you watch your weight. Excess takes its toll one way or another. Since this book is chiefly an attempt to explain, we are not concerned with condemning intemperance. We can only state the facts and leave the individual to make an independent decision.

The same applies to smoking, but within a slightly different context. Authorities differ about the relationship between lung cancer and smoking, and smokers and anti-smokers believe whatever supports their case. There is no positive proof that smoking causes cancer, but there is strong evidence of a connection. The incidence of lung cancer is greater among heavy smokers than among light smokers, and greater among light smokers than among non-smokers. More cigarette smokers than pipe smokers or cigar smokers develop lung cancer. The published figures are alarming and deserve to be taken seriously.

The lung cancer issue is controversial and you can please yourself which side to believe, but there is no doubt among doctors about the adverse effect of smoking on heart and chest. Cigarette smoking raises the blood pressure and increases liability to coronary thrombosis. Smoker's cough is a warning, generally unheeded, of the injury to the respiratory function. We know a man who goes down with bronchitis regularly every autumn, stays at home under doctor's orders, and continues smoking against doctor's orders to relieve the tedium. 'Well, you've got to do something, haven't you?' he says belligerently.

If you have got to do something, and smoking is the only recourse, all health arguments will fail. For heavy cigarette smokers the choice may be whether to suffer with or without the habit. They can try switching to a pipe and avoid the added risk from inhaling. But the only true safeguard is to stop smoking.

Breaking the habit is of course less of a wrench for moderate smokers and non-inhalers, but it is not easy for anyone. Smoking is escapist, as is drinking. It soothes the nerves and, in excess, blurs life's problems. There is no standard prescription or procedure for breaking the habit. Some people can reduce consumption and resist relapses. Some find it possible to cut down gradually to total abstinence. A few, either more heroic or less addicted, stop abruptly and for good. In any case it takes a few weeks to lose the craving. The most puzzling cases are the very few who stop smoking completely and successfully, and after months or even years resume without reason. They defy comment.

7
Looking after Yourself

In less complicated times it used to be said that after forty every man is either a fool or a physician. Like most folk aphorisms which rely on exaggeration to make their point, it contains some truth and much scope for misunderstanding. If it led to self-medication it was of doubtful value in those days and could be disastrous in ours. The fools may be the lay physicians.

Knowledge about health has increased enormously and so have treatments. The number and variety of drugs have multiplied. Some are potent remedies for once intractable diseases, and can have unpleasant side effects. Even familiar pain-killers, which used to be thought harmless, are now prescribed with warnings against excessive use. The patient is less and less of a physician.

Advances in medicine are helping people to live longer. While perhaps not increasing the human span, they can help to prolong the individual's life to something nearer its potential limit. An obvious consequence, as we said earlier, is that the old and retired constitute an ever larger proportion of the population. Another is that people are living long enough to suffer from the diseases and disabilities of old age, which a generation or two ago they might have escaped by early death.

These circumstances place two important obligations upon the old. First, to recognize which symptoms are due to easily corrected errors in living or to a condition which has to be lived with, and those which indicate a need for medical advice. Second, to live sensibly and take care to avoid, as far as possible, physical injury and breakdown in health.

Let us consider the second one first. There is an intelligent middle way between giving in too easily to the difficulties of old age and knowing when to accept the facts of ageing. It is no use fighting the inevitable. There are many things you can't hope to do at seventy that you took in your stride at fifty, and you must have noticed a similar decline between thirty and fifty. Acceptance is easier if the signs of age are unmistakeable. It can be rather depressing if you seem fit and strong for your age.

It is true that people age at different rates. Some are old at fifty, some a youthful seventy. But fitness in the later years can be deceptive. You may be better than the average of your age group, but there has been a falling off. Your muscles are softer, your bones are brittle, your reactions slower, your body less nimble, you tire more easily, your heart and lungs do not recover so quickly from exertion. You may not look or feel your age, but sixty or seventy years of hard wear, without benefit of spare parts, take their toll of one's organs.

However you feel, you should give age the benefit of the doubt. If you don't, you will learn the truth the hard way. You sprint a hundred yards for a bus and pant as though you had done an Olympic mile. You paint two ceilings in a morning and your arms weigh a hundred-weight each. You lift some heavy pieces of furniture and you can't unbend next morning. You let yourself get overtired, because you don't like to admit to younger people that you will have to drop out. But there's no disgrace in knowing your limitations.

You are limited by your past experience as well as your present age. If you have been a removals man or an athlete you will continue to be stronger than the average person of your age. But even strong men have to slow down with advancing years.

EXERCISE IN MODERATION

Avoid the extremes of bravado and timidity and look after yourself. We have had a good deal to say about diet, and especially the weight problem. Exercise will help to keep your weight level. But don't expect too much of physical activity. While lack of exercise can soon add pounds to your weight, you won't lose them by exercise. Elderly people can't take a morning run round the houses or a work-out in a gymnasium. Sweating out the surplus fat could cause the very injury that dieting is intended to avert.

Exercise has other merits. It tones the muscles, expands the lungs, stimulates the heart. If you are used to outdoor sports, carry on within reason. But if you are not, and you think you would like to start now

C

that retirement has given you time, be careful. Unaccustomed physical exertion can be harmful if you try to do too much too soon. Increase the effort gradually and slow down if it becomes a strain.

Don't overdo the exercise

You will remember that our hypothetical planner phased out the more strenuous sports as he approached retirement. He continued to enjoy swimming and added bowls to his repertoire. He had to fight down a prejudice against bowls, which used to be considered an old person's game. At about his time, though, it was becoming popular among younger people too. It is one of the more accessible outdoor sports; most districts have a nearby park with a bowling green.

Exercise that can be taken only on location is a limited indulgence, but walking is available at your doorstep at any time. Everyone except cripples and invalids should do some walking. Yet it is surprising how many mobile people neglect this simple, cheap and healthful exercise. The chief offenders are car slaves and retired people. Car slaves will walk miles on the golf course but drive a couple of hundred yards to the corner shop. Retired people, no longer obliged to walk to the bus or station, often refuse to bother and go no further than the bottom of the garden.

Even those who don't mind walking usually want an objective. Walking for walking's sake (which means for health's sake) need not be a bore. Many men go shopping with their wives and help to push the trolley home. But for days when there is nowhere special to go, one has to create interests to dispel the tedium of the familiar circuit of library, post office, bank and park.

The monotony may be in ourselves more than in the neighbourhood. There is always something happening in any locality, trivial perhaps but adding seasoning to the walk if you train yourself to notice. Old established shops close down and new ones start up. A pretentious semi-detached house suddenly sports a stately home type of portico. The landscape acquires a new look when a clump of elms is cut down. Derelict houses are demolished to make a car park. Or the walk may yield a more human interest and half an hour's conversation if an acquaintance passes your way.

You can explore the area more widely. When the immediate neighbourhood palls have a walk in another a bus-ride away: you have your pass. There may be attractive old buildings, new developments you have read about in your local newspaper, or the site of a controversial borough project. You bring back talking points.

Make it a rule to walk every day. Even if you are a keen gardener you need to stretch your legs. Don't let the weather deter you if you are fit and well protected. There is no need to make your walk a ritual or to count the miles and hours. Your body will tell you how much is enough.

Of course if you are a dog lover there is no problem. His needs will take priority over yours. He will take you for a walk.

Walking, gardening and sport act upon most muscles, but some escape, as you discover when an unaccustomed exertion leaves you with an ache in a shoulder or calf. You don't need elaborate drill to tone up those muscles. There are simple exercises which can be carried out at odd moments without equipment or training. Many can be done sitting down or in the bath. They are gentle, safe, and in some ways more effective than the trials of strength and endurance we suffered in the school gym.

These exercises are known as isometrics. They are not new or revolutionary. They had been known and practised long before they were adopted and systematized in the 1960s by the American marines. By simple pushing, pulling and squeezing exercises you can strengthen your muscles in your own time and within your limits.

One of these exercises is specially for the abdominal muscles. While standing at the bus stop, or in the kitchen, or looking in a shop window, pull your abdomen in, hold the position for a few seconds, then push out. Repeat half a dozen times. You can combine this with a breathing exercise. Breathe in and push the abdomen out, hold for a second, then breathe out and pull the muscles in. This exercise, practised two or three times a day, corrects or reduces a paunch, and assists digestion and bowel action.

Arms and legs can also benefit from push/pull techniques. Stand eighteen inches from a rigid object such as a wall or door frame. With right foot forward place your right palm on the wall and push hard. Repeat with left foot forward and left palm pushing. Then with shoes off, put the soles of your feet alternately flat against the wall and push.

You can do the hand pushing downwards with any movable object – broom, vacuum cleaner, kitchen stool – against a hard floor. In other exercises legs and arms co-operate. Brace your feet against the table legs from a seated position, grasp the sides of the table with your hands and try to pull it towards you.

There are other ways of competing with yourself. Clasp your hands across your chest, push them together, then try to pull them apart. While sitting in a straight-backed chair, grasp your right leg with both hands under the knee, and against the leg's resistance pull it up towards your chest. Repeat with the left leg. Still sitting, grasp the seat on each side of you and press hard downwards as if trying to raise yourself on your hands. Then put your hands under the seat on each side and pull upwards as though trying to lift yourself and the chair.

In addition there are old fashioned leg and toe exercises which are still effective. Stand with hands on hips and raise yourself on your toes, holding the position for a few seconds. While seated raise each leg off the ground and wiggle the toes up and down. Again while sitting, press each foot alternately against the ground as if marking time. Lying on your back in bed or on the floor raise your legs and move them as if pedalling a bicycle for a few seconds. Foot and leg exercises are easier and less tiring if done under water. The water gives buoyancy without weakening the result.

Another kind of exercise is to stand behind a chair, grasp the back on each side, and press your hands towards each other as if trying to crush the chair. To strengthen hands and fingers, try to tear a discarded telephone directory apart, but without any ambition to emulate a strong-man result. The possibilities of isometric exercises are limitless. You can think of others for yourself.

For the best results you should exercise regularly. Starting enthusiastically and losing interest after a few days will do no good. Neither will desultory exercising, taken up when you remember. Choose a time – before breakfast or between meals morning or afternoon – and as far as possible develop a routine. Arrange a sequence of exercises to to suit yourself.

Don't overdo the exercises. A few minutes at a time should be enough. One of their chief merits is that they are non-competitive. Nobody is forcing the pace. The choice of what, when and how much rests with you. If you find the exercises tiring reduce the frequency. If one of them, say the pedalling, makes you dizzy, drop it.

Exercises for the neck and back require great care. Do them gently, without jerks or twists. Move the head from side to side, raise it up and down, bend the neck left then right. With hands on hips bend the body forward and back, then to the left and right, then swing the trunk left and right. But if you feel the slightest twinge or strain, stop at once. The backbone, as the body's main prop, is very vulnerable in older people. Damage caused in a moment may take months to repair.

Beware of trying to emulate the prowess of exceptional people. In 1976 the playwright Mr Ben Travers, near his ninetieth birthday, demonstrated a feat on television that must have shamed lesser men of half his age. He lay flat on his back, raised his legs, and three times in swift succession touched the floor behind his head with his toes. Even after a lifelong practice of physical culture, it was an astonishing performance. But for other elderly people a phenomenon is not exemplary. One can't go back fifty years and start body-building. It might not help if one could. Some of us were unable even to touch our toes as schoolboys. You can't be a Ben Travers, but you can, with body care, attain a higher level within your capacity.

Posture is no less important than exercise. Old people sag and become round-shouldered, sometimes because of softening of the bones in old age, but in many cases because they stand badly. Standing and walking with the back straight (but not poker-straight) rests the weight of the body comfortably on its central column. Deviation from that position strains the back and tends to pull it down. You can prove this easily. Hold a spade vertically in one hand, then tilt it slightly forward, and note how the apparent weight increases.

Lounging is bad for the back. The standard easy chair is insidiously easy. It encourages curvatures while giving a false sense of repose. A straight-backed chair with a cushion is best for ageing backs – and for younger ones too.

A soft sagging mattress is another postural menace. It feels like heaven when you go to bed tired, and when you wake tired you attribute that fact to anything but the spine-curving mattress. Doctors prescribe a firm mattress for people with back troubles. It is also the right prescription for people who want to avoid back troubles.

Sitting cross-legged is another deceptively easeful posture. It constricts the veins and can cause fatigue and cramp. Circulation becomes more sluggish with age. Circulatory conditions such as varicose veins and phlebitis are more common in the old than in the young. It is advisable not to sit too long with the legs in one position, but to stretch them from time to time and occasionally take a turn round the room.

Many of these precepts are based on fairly common knowledge. You may be practising them already. They are offered here as reminders.

SAFETY FOR THE OLD

Even careful people need reminding about safety. Physical balance deteriorates with age. You are not so secure on a ladder at seventy-five as you were at sixty. Deterioration is gradual, you may not become aware of it until you actually suffer a fall. Therefore watch your step. Be careful at any age over sixty if you have to stand on a chair. Make sure that the chair is steady, with all four legs on the same level. In the later seventies and after, give up climbing. Get someone younger to reach for the top shelf or, preferably, keep things within easier reach.

Look out for trip wires. Better still, remember not to leave trailing flex or obstacles in places when you might fall over them. Discard torn slippers; have torn carpets and rugs repaired. Tread warily on broken pavements. Take stairs at home and elsewhere slowly and hold on to the rail. Everyone knows that a fall is more serious when age has made bones brittle and has diminished healing power.

Old people are liable to fall from other causes than carelessness. Legs can give way or faintness can occur without warning. If you are subject to dizziness avoid sudden movements or change of position. If you have to bend, straighten out slowly and hold on to something till the giddy feeling caused by blood flowing back from the head has subsided.

Be careful how you cross a busy road. Mental reactions become more sluggish with age and you are not physically as nimble as you were. It makes sense to wait for the lights or walk a few yards further on to cross on an island. These concessions to the facts of ageing should not be felt as a defeat. Defiance would not be a sign of determination but of obstinacy.

Should you continue to drive? And how late in life? That is a more difficult question. A fraction of a second's delay in your reaction to sudden danger can mean disaster for you or another person. A pedestrian can take precautions and evasive actions which are not available to a motorist. Roads are becoming more congested daily, and it is not always possible to bypass the heavy traffic. You will have to rely on your experience as a motorist of long standing and on your judgement of your fitness to drive. A near miss for which you cannot wholly blame the other driver will be a warning. But you should not wait for shocks. If you have to take medicines which slow you down, or your distant vision is becoming unreliable, ask your doctor and your oculist to say frankly whether you should continue to drive. After the age of seventy, ask them in any case, each time you go for a check-up.

Like mental reactions, physical faculties gradually weaken. The sense of smell is less acute in the old, and a gas leakage less easily detected. One has to guard against absence of mind in handling gas fires and cookers. The sense of taste is also less keen, and the risk of poisoning from food contamination is increased. Remember also that smoking impairs both taste and smell. If you cannot rely on your senses for safety, you have to be extra careful not to keep food long enough to deteriorate. Better be over-cautious than over-confident. One of the problems of ageing is that nature tends to make us less alert when the need for vigilance is greatest.

Sleep poses new problems in old age. Insomnia is not peculiar to the old, but it is generally true that they need less sleep than younger people. If you have a nap during the day you cannot expect to sleep through the night. Some people sleep better after a nightcap of hot milk, others find that any liquid taken within an hour of bedtime increases the likelihood of waking to empty the bladder. You have to experiment to find your own remedies for wakefulness. If you can get by with little sleep, you will have to find an occupation for the waking hours that will not disturb others in the house – reading, or a game of patience, or some quiet household job.

Insomnia is a wretched condition and sleeping tablets offer release. Too many people yield too readily, and some doctors are too free with prescriptions. If you are not happy about artificial aids, ask your doctor what he thinks. When they are prescribed in illness you may have no choice. Otherwise you have to decide whether the risk of addiction is preferable to the misery of many wakeful hours night after night.

In winter you will sleep better with the window shut. There is an old English myth that plenty of fresh air is good for you at all seasons and in all circumstances. In fact, many creatures sleep better without fresh air. Nature provides many examples. Cats sleep with nose covered and birds with beak under a wing. Human beings get drowsy in a fug for lack of oxygen. While bad air is not recommended, a reduced intake of stimulating oxygen does assist sleep.

A cold and draughty environment has special dangers for the old. One's internal thermostat becomes less efficient with age, and body temperature can easily fall to a point beyond the possibility of recovery. This condition is known as hypothermia. Elderly people can die of cold in temperatures that are not very low by ordinary standards.

Adequate food and a warm home are safeguards against hypothermia. They should be among the highest priorities of life in retirement. They are also among the highest cost items and liable to be skimped by the poorer majority. As far as possible, keep the house at an even temperature throughout. You will realize the need if you have to go from a warm bed to a chilly toilet at night.

Dress warmly but don't overdo the wrappings. Elderly ladies are more prone than men to wear unnecessary layers of clothing. On the other hand, don't sacrifice comfort to fashion. If your bald head shrinks from the icy blast, wear a hat, even if your Spartan friends go hatless. By the time you retire you are old enough to break out of conventions. In matters of warmth your body should be the arbiter. If it cries out for wool it will not be happy with synthetics.

Precautions against accidents and breakdown in health should become part of your way of life, but not a morbid preoccupation. The elderly are not invalids but they become progressively less robust and more damageable. For that reason they are more often in need of medical attention. The relationship between patient and doctor may change with age.

An overworked doctor finds many of his aged patients something of a trial. They have vague symptoms which they find difficult to express in words. Some want cures or relief for conditions which are an irremediable consequence of growing old. Others neglect to report certain symptoms through fear of what they may be told and so aggravate the condition. Those who are neither hypochondriac nor stupid still need to know when and when not to consult the doctor.

Most of the fugitive aches and pains in ageing bones and muscles can be ignored. Any undue strain – strap-hanging for a long journey, carrying a heavy case, jerking a shoulder or knee in preventing a fall – can cause pains which may last for days, weeks or even months. If they gradually improve, you just have to be patient. If they persist and movement is painful you will be justified in getting medical advice.

Between running to the doctor with every little trouble and dosing yourself because you think you know best, there is room for judgement and self-restraint. Don't take other people's medicines. They may have been prescribed for a different condition and could do you harm. Take a pain-killer for the occasional headache but beware of continual dosing. Aspirin can cause damage if you have gastric trouble, paracetamol is not as harmless as it was once thought to be. There is no such thing as a completely safe pain-killer. Get your doctor's advice about frequent use.

If you are given a course of treatment, carry it through to the end. Don't stop taking the prescribed tablets because you feel better already. The trouble will return. It takes the whole treatment to knock out the bugs. Don't try to get back into your stride too soon after serious illness such as a coronary or a stroke. The doctor will say when. Younger people can sometimes take chances successfully. There may be no second chance for the old.

Try to be co-operative with your doctor and treat him with consideration. Like most other doctors he has suffered from the abuse of the National Health Service by the unscrupulous and the neurotic.

Do you think you should have a medical overhaul when you retire? Some find it reassuring to start a new life with a new bill of health. Unless your condition requires it, you may find it easier to procure a general check-up as a private patient than under the National Health Service, because it takes more time than most general practitioners can spare. If you are on good terms with your doctor he may agree to arrange a general examination.

He will help in more urgent cases too. The family doctor is the channel for obtaining hospital treatment, home help in sickness and convalescence, and aids for the physically handicapped.

EYES, EARS AND TEETH

No doubt you already have a long-standing arrangement with an oculist and a dentist. Unless you are one of the lucky few with vision unimpaired you will have discovered in middle age what the years do to your eyes. You may already be wearing bifocals, and will know how you have to watch your step when going downstairs. Eyes grow old like other parts of the body. Like them, they are vulnerable to disease, but unlike the teeth they don't wear out. Some oculists say that you can no more strain your eyes with reading than your ears with listening. But the eyes do tire more easily with age and the vision suffers deterioration.

Whether we call the condition strain or fatigue, tired or aching eyes should be rested. Palming for ten or fifteen minutes to exclude light, and at the same time imagining a completely black background, helps the eyes to recover from too much application. Old eyes need a good light for reading and close work. They water more than the eyes of the young, and should not be exposed too long to a cold wind. Glasses need changing from time to time as the eyes become less efficient. Your oculist or optician should remind you when he thinks a test is due. While you may not suffer damage to your eyes by delaying a test or a change of glasses, you will be less comfortable and more accident prone with uncorrected vision.

Ears grow old as the eyes do and the results are comparable – a dimming and distorting of the faculty. But the patient's attitude to defective hearing is different. Glasses are accepted more philosophic-ally than a hearing aid. Women hesitate through vanity, men because it seems like a conspicuous surrender to the ultimate enemy. In fact, you can't escape the enemy by pretending the deficiency doesn't exist. Failing to hear makes you more conspicuous than wearing an aid.

Don't go to the other extreme and buy an advertised hearing aid on the assumption that your hearing is impaired. Your doctor may find that you only need to have your ears syringed to clear an accumu-lation of wax. If you do need an aid you can have one without charge under the NHS, or you can buy a proprietary model. Let your doctor advise.

Some users take more kindly than others to a hearing aid. The older you are the more difficult it becomes to make the adjustment. It is worth-while to persevere. Deafness is a lonely and socially inhibiting condition.

Look after your teeth, whether provided by nature or the dentist. If you have some of your own left, your dentist will remind you period-ically to come for a check-up. He may not do so if you wear dentures only. In that case you should arrange a visit every four or five years.

Gums shrink, the mouth changes shape, and dentures become loose and painful. In order to avoid pain you may either fail to chew adequately and get indigestion, or eat slops without your teeth and become undernourished. There is also an aesthetic reason for dental care. People are repelled by false teeth that wobble and click when you talk.

The most neglected parts of the body seem to be at each end. The old often complain that their feet are 'killing' them, but do nothing to get relief. The first essential is to have comfortable shoes. Don't grudge the cost. Go to a shop which employs fitters, in preference to the growing number that offer self-service and possibly self-crippling. A good fit is much more important in shoes than in a coat, though judging by their actions many people seem to think otherwise.

Heavyweight people obviously put excessive strain on ankles and feet — another good reason for keeping your weight down. Keep toenails trimmed and have corns and callouses expertly treated. Damage to the feet can be serious in elderly people. If you need chiropody your doctor may be able to arrange it through the NHS.

With timely attention most of the physical disabilities of age can be mitigated. Others are so integral a part of the ageing process as to be beyond help. One of the most distressing is impairment of memory. The breakdown of the bodily functions is easier to tolerate than that of the mind. You forget (perhaps temporarily) names, dates, past events and things you intended to do. It is not merely embarrassing. It is a source of danger. You may switch on the gas and omit to light it, forget to lock up at night, mislay your keys, forget you have taken a potent tablet and repeat the dose.

Since there is no cure for memory failure you must fall back on the obvious expedients. Keep a diary and carry a notebook. Write reminders for yourself and display them where you can't miss them. Write down everything you intend to say before telephoning, and save a second call. Carry a shopping list, though only three or four items long. Keep a note of the whereabouts of documents and other items in your house — and pray you won't forget where you have put the note.

Apart from names and words, which will elude you whatever you do, you can avoid much brain-racking by means of method and habit. Keep things where they have always been so that retrieval is almost instinctive. Out of place, out of mind, is a useful variant of an old maxim.

So far we have dealt with health matters which you can understand and do something about yourself. There are, however, symptoms of more mysterious troubles which may indicate the start of a serious condition, and should be referred to your doctor without delay. These are unexpected and inexplicable changes in bodily conditions and functions. For instance, if you suffer habitually from digestive and bowel irregularities you won't be alarmed by occasional acidity or wind, or a bout of diarrhoea or constipation. But if you have always been regular you will need to know what has caused the change. If you cough up or pass blood, if you develop a lump anywhere (in women, commonly, in the breast), if a skin eruption doesn't heal, if you have a sudden loss of vision or prolonged pain in an eye, if you have pain in the chest which you can't attribute to indigestion, go to your doctor.

For your convenience we have listed some symptoms that need to be taken seriously. But first, a warning. Don't panic if you develop what might appear to be alarming symptoms. And don't delay reporting them for fear of the worst. They may indicate a non-dangerous condition or one which can be made safe by prompt attention. Don't run to medical books to make your own diagnosis. Your doctor will establish the facts by examination.

Some of the items in the checklist will apply to men, some to women only, but most will concern both sexes. That is true of everything that has been said in this book, except where we have particularized the circumstances, problems and needs of women.

CHECKLIST

	Symptoms	Indications
Abdomen	Severe pain and tenderness on pressure.	Different from the griping pain and discomfort which is relieved by bowel action. Could indicate disease of gall bladder, appendix, duodenum, or bowel, and may require emergency surgery.
	Swelling in or near groin which subsides when you are lying down.	Sign of hernia. Will require control by truss or repair by surgery.
Arms	Severe pain along the arms usually accompanied by pain in the chest.	May point to angina or coronary thrombosis. Should receive immediate medical attention.

	Symptoms	Indications
Back	Pain at the base of the spine.	May be muscular or organic. See your doctor if rest does not bring relief.
Bladder	Difficulty in passing urine.	Sometimes due to faecal obstruction in constipation. Commonly caused, in men, by enlarged prostate.
	Frequent urination.	Should be tested for prostate trouble or infection.
	Pain in urination.	Common in women, particularly, as indicating cystitis. Occasionally due to stone in the bladder.
	Blood in urine.	A possible sign of kidney failure or of a growth (not necessarily malignant) in the bladder. Report promptly to your doctor.
Bowels	Constipation and diarrhoea.	Some people are habitually liable to constipation, and anyone can have the odd attack of diarrhoea, without cause for worry; but any unfamiliar and inexplicable change in bowel action should be reported promptly to your doctor.
	Very dark or black faeces.	This is normal if you are taking iron medicine, but if not due to medication or diet it is likely to be caused by duodenal bleeding. Go promptly to your doctor.
	Bleeding from the rectum.	Could be due to piles or more serious trouble. Requires prompt medical attention.
Breast	A lump, however small. Indrawn or inverted nipple, or bleeding or discharge from nipple.	Could indicate a benign or malignant growth. Seek prompt medical attention.
Chest	Pain on exertion, or any pain not attributable to indigestion.	Pain which resolves spontaneously should still receive prompt attention. If it is severe and does not resolve itself, it needs immediate attention.

	Symptoms	Indications
Chest (cont.)	Cough.	Heavy smokers recognize smokers' cough. The only cure is to reduce or stop smoking. Any other cough which persists for three or four weeks should be reported to the doctor. Coughing up blood should be reported promptly.
Ears	Discharge from the ear.	Due to infection which can usually be treated successfully.
	Deafness.	The doctor will syringe the ears, and, if that fails, will recommend a hearing aid.
Eyes	Floaters.	These floating specks are not a sign of impaired vision or disease, and should be ignored.
	Pain in the eyes, blurred vision, haloes round lights, flashes or double vision.	May indicate something more serious than a functional change, possibly cataract or glaucoma or brain tumour, requiring surgical treatment. Go to your doctor promptly.
Feet & legs	Corns and hard skin.	Should be treated by a chiropodist and not by oneself.
	Painful and discoloured feet.	Usually a sign of poor circulation. Should be reported to your doctor.
	Ulcerations of or damage to the feet, and ingrowing toenails.	Self-treatment can be harmful. Report to your doctor.
	Swelling of ankles.	May indicate circulatory or cardiac defect, which can be treated.
	Pain in the calf.	Possibly due to defective circulation or varicose veins (especially in women who have had children). Varicose veins can cause ulcers if neglected, but can be controlled, either by stockings or, better, by surgery.
Genitals	Irritation or rash on the skin in the genital area.	Itching on any part of the body may be a warning of infection or diabetes. Report to your doctor.

	Symptoms	Indications
	Swelling of the scrotum.	Could be a result of hernia, requiring surgery.
	Bleeding or other discharge from the vagina.	Should have immediate medical attention.
Hands	Pain and stiffness, with swelling or deformation of the joints.	Usually indicates arthritis. Treatment should be sought if it is troublesome.
	Numbness and tingling of hands and other parts of the body.	There could be a variety of causes, most of them not serious, but the condition should not be ignored.
	Tremor.	Trembling of the hands is a feature of ageing for which there is no treatment, but ask your doctor to check that nothing more serious, such as Parkinson's disease, is present.
Head	Severe or recurring head pains differing from any headache with which you are familiar.	May indicate a variety of illness. You should seek prompt medical attention. The doctor will test your blood pressure, advise an eye test, enquire about any injury you may have sustained, or seek the cause in some change in your habits and way of life.
	Dizziness.	If persistent, should not be accepted as one of the disabilities of ageing, but reported to your doctor. (He will probably tell you that it is just old age.)
Heart	(Also see chest.) Pains.	Angina can be controlled with drugs; coronary thrombosis may require a long rest and treatment. Neither need leave you an invalid. A reasonable amount of exercise after recovery will strengthen the heart muscles, but smoking must stop and your weight must be kept down to the average for your age and build.

	Symptoms	*Indications*
Joints	(Also see *hands.*) Stiffness.	Inevitable in the later years, but can be alleviated with light exercise.
	Pain and swelling of the joints.	There are two kinds of arthritis, both of which can be crippling. Except in the most extreme cases something can be done on medical advice to reduce pain and maintain mobility. Excessive weight puts additional strain on arthritic knees and ankles. The artificial hip joint has completely changed the outlook for people crippled by arthritis in the hips; but at present no other joints can be successfully replaced.
Lungs	(Also see *chest.*) Pains.	Difficulty or pain in breathing, and spitting or coughing blood, should be reported to your doctor without delay. Shortness of breath on exercise may be due to heart failure and may be treatable.
Mouth	Excessive dryness of the mouth, soreness of mouth and tongue, or abnormal thirst.	May point to organic disorders which require medical treatment.
	Sore gums.	Could be due to infection or badly fitting dentures. You can usually recognize which. Try your dentist first.
	Sense of taste.	Deteriorates inevitably with age. Smoking makes things worse.
Nose	Sense of smell.	Less acute in old people. Reduced still further by smoking.
	Blocked nose.	If persistent and not accompanied by a cold, this is probably chronic catarrh. Don't fly to advertised remedies but seek your doctor's advice.

	Symptoms	Indications
	Spots and soreness inside the nose.	Infections in the nose can be troublesome, and if persistent should be cleared up as the doctor directs.
	Bleeding from the nose.	Not necessarily a safety valve as it is sometimes supposed to be. Repeated and copious nose bleeds should be reported to your doctor.
Skin	(Also see genitals.) Irritation or rash.	Itching areas and rashes that don't clear up quickly can be due to a variety of causes calling for medical diagnosis.
	Spots and moles.	If a spot grows or bleeding starts in a mole or other skin blemish report promptly to your doctor.
Stomach	(Also see abdomen.) Wind, heartburn, heaviness not due to over-eating.	If these are new in your experience and persistent, tell your doctor.
	Vomiting blood.	Could indicate gastric ulcer or impending extreme loss of blood which could be fatal. Report immediately to your doctor, or get an ambulance to take you to hospital.
Strokes	Sudden or gradual onset of difficulty in speaking or in moving an arm or leg. Sudden loss of consciousness.	Should receive immediate medical attention and may require hospital admission. With physiotherapy and speech therapy, complete recovery is possible; but it is a long haul and may take months.
Throat	Difficulty in swallowing. Soreness and pain, whether or not caused by a cold, and not clearing up within two or three weeks. Hoarseness of voice not attributable to heavy smoking.	All these conditions are cases for medical advice.

There a few conditions that do not fit logically into a list based on parts of the body. One of these is loss of appetite – not just a reduction in the amount of food needed, but a complete loss of interest in food. The cause may be the all-too-common apathy of the old, or the boredom of catering for oneself and eating alone. But sometimes the condition may be psychological and not possible to correct by an act of will. Your doctor must find the deeper cause.

Any extreme change in weight requires medical advice. We have talked about overweight and its treatment. But continuous unaccountable loss of weight is more puzzling. The cause may be psychological, or the weight loss may indicate organic disease. It is not a heaven-sent opportunity to slim.

Persistent depression is not uncommon in old people. It may be an understandable reaction to ill health, domestic troubles and lack of money, or it may be an illness in its own right. Have a frank talk with your doctor. He will need to ask a number of personal questions in tracing the cause, and you should regard these as legitimate aids to diagnosis, like questions about your stomach and bowels. He will take you more seriously than your friends, and not simply tell you to pull yourself together.

Extreme tiredness is another condition that should be taken seriously. It is easily distinguished from the diminution of strength and energy which are normal as one grows older. It may be due to anaemia which can be treated successfully, or to a more complicated cause which your doctor should be able to diagnose.

A time comes in the process of ageing when you find yourself getting short of breath. If you have been pounding up the hills at your old pace and your breath returns when you slow down, you know the remedy. So you do if you reduce your smoking and find you breathe better. But respiratory troubles can have many other causes (chronic bronchitis, emphysema or heart disease) which you cannot guess at for yourself. If moderate exertion makes you puff excessively ask your doctor what is wrong.

A question which has worried many elderly people has been whether sexual activity should continue into the later years. Some people have believed it could be harmful, but have been restrained by early inhibitions from asking their doctor. The medical answer today is that it can do no harm and may actually be beneficial. With this fear out of the way, it becomes a matter for the two partners themselves to decide.

8

A Working Retirement

In retiremen₁ you have more free time than ever before in your adult life. Forty hours and more a week, formerly contracted to an employer, are back on your hands. That's a lot of time to fill, either with work or play.

Unless you are one of the very few who can be happy doing nothing, you will want to be active. A large part of the activity will be work. Man (and that includes woman) is a working animal – the only working animal apart from those he sets to work. He may hate what he has to do for a living, but will cheerfully slave on a self-imposed task in the home. He enjoys work for its own sake, no matter what other reasons there may be.

Statistics prove the necessity of work. Nearly fifty per cent of men continue to work after sixty-five, about a third are still working at seventy and a quarter at seventy-five. We have all known men and women who have been gainfully employed at eighty or over.

Work in retirement can be paid or unpaid. Unpaid work is either voluntary, i.e. undertaken for others, or personal, for one's own enjoyment. You will probably choose activities in all three sectors. This chapter and the two following will discuss the possibilities.

If you have planned your retirement, you will have made some provision for using your extra leisure. Look again at our specimen personal audit. The planner listed his interests and capabilities. His job had involved some draughtsmanship and technical photography, and these led to scenic photography and sketching. He was mechanically minded and one of nature's handymen. He enjoyed gardening, he liked people, was a good teamsman, and considered doing voluntary work for charity. Other activities – reading, theatre and sport – were a continuation, with some modification, of his old interests.

Some people don't retire at all

One of the advantages of planning is that it helps you to make the right decision. Your leisure may be abundant, but it is not limitless. Neither is your energy. Without a plan you may be tempted to under-take more than you can fulfil. If you are on your own you can absorb your mistakes. But if you are working for or with others, the outcome may be frustrating for them and humiliating for yourself.

You will have to take other costs into account. A commitment may be attractive but could prove more expensive than you had thought. Or it may clash with another regular assignment, or make excessive demands on your strength. In planning you will view every prospect in the light of your means, skills, health, energy, character, tempera-ment and, not least, available time.

Unless you have one absorbing and inexhaustible interest, you will aim at variety and balance. You will want to exercise mind and body. You will intersperse the heavier activities with some slight and frivolous ones. You will do some things alone, and share others with your wife and perhaps with a group. You will be wise to leave some time for the odd job or impulse, or just for enjoyable idling.

That is not as big a programme as it might seem. You will obviously space out your activities. Some will be regular, some occasional. A personal plan can be flexible, allowing for additions, deletions and changes of mind. The basic fact about a plan is, we repeat, that it must be better than no plan. It saves you from drifting, and so wasting the precious leisure you have worked a lifetime to gain.

You may decide upon a major activity to fill perhaps half of the gap left by giving up full-time paid employment. As we pointed out in an earlier chapter some people find retirement exhilarating and want a complete change, while others find it disturbing and, for a time at least, want continuity. True continuity may not be possible. Some kinds of work are inseparable from the plant and processes involved. You can't take any part of highly automated machining, assembly or control work with you into retirement. But there are other ways of retaining the comfortable sense of involvement in the working world.

OPPORTUNITY FOR WORK

One way is to seek opportunities for part-time work at your former place of employment. You can make it part of your retirement planning to explore the possibilities. The work will probably be different from what you have been doing, but will be within your capabilities. You may be able to suggest a service which had not occurred to the management. In a few organizations – too few, you might think – the management is enlightened enough to look for ways of retaining the services of experienced employees about to retire.

Here is a case known to us. The manager of a company's transport fleet, at the age of retirement, was fully capable of continuing on the job, and the company's retirement policy was not inflexible. But there was a competent deserving second-in-command due for promotion, and a string of climbers on the ladder below him. The chairman found a solution that satisfied everyone. The company was an exporter, and often had visitors from overseas who had to be met and accommodated. Some of these visitors were no longer young. They would appreciate being welcomed by an older man who would understand their needs and look after their comforts. The retired transport manager was an admirable and willing choice for this delicate job of customer relations.

However resourceful the top management may be, such opportunities would be rare in any organization. But many managements are open to suggestion. If you have taken part in a company's Suggestion Scheme you will be in the habit of looking for ways of improving products, methods and procedures. You could use this kind of initiative on a new proposition, yourself.

Those who find part-time employment in the old firm after official retirement are in a special category. So are the self-employed. They decide for themselves when to retire. Some do not retire at all. For those who do, the transition is often so gradual as to be imperceptible. A watch repairer can accept work as long as his vision remains clear and his hand steady. A decorator need not give up while he can trust himself on a ladder. An insurance agent, a self-employed typist, a freelance journalist can carry on as long and as busily as the market for their services allows.

There remains a large body of people for whom retirement is a clean break with paid employment. If they want to earn some money they must start afresh. Only the very few are fortunate enough to have substantial indexed pensions which keep well above the national average earnings. The rest are either poor, or worried about the inadequacy of a fixed income against rising costs. Paid work for them is not simply a means of keeping happily active. They need the money.

In those circumstances you have to find answers to three questions. What are the prospects for paid work? What kind of work shall I do? Where can I go for advice?

But first, you must face some hard facts. If you want work you must go out and get it. Jobs will not come to you. The world did not owe you a living when you were young. It does not owe you paid work in retirement. There may be people who can help you or who can use your services. But they don't know of your existence or your need. You have to let people know what you can do and what you want. In short, put yourself up for hire.

And don't imagine that it will be easy. You will be competing with people in employment and a long queue of the unemployed. They are all younger than you. However grim the situation may be, they have a better chance than you at the employment exchange and through the jobs vacant columns. Up to the day before retirement you were obviously still employable. The day after retirement you became, in the eyes of the general run of employers, unemployable.

This is not a case for despair, but for realism and enterprise. You have to offer a service, perhaps locally, that bigger operators cannot or will not tackle, and that is not over-supplied by one-man operators like yourself. It will be a development of your employment experience or of a skilled leisure activity. You will make sure that it does not involve you in a bigger commitment or capital outlay than you can reasonably afford.

For instance, if you have worked on the technical side of the electrical industry you might get your name on the service list of a local electrical dealer. He will probably be too small to employ a full time electrician, but will be glad to have a reliable freelance whom he can recommend to customers. The work will be intermittent and will sometimes clash with your leisure interests. But if you want the money you must pay the price.

You can expand the work in two directions. One is geographical. You can have cards printed and drop them into people's letterboxes a little beyond your immediate locality. The other is technical. You may not have handled household electrical equipment (vacuum cleaners, televisions, washing machines), but with a little study you might add some of them to your repertoire.

Anyone who has worked on accounts can similarly offer a service to local traders. Shopkeepers, small builders and decorators are overwhelmed with paperwork and might welcome help with VAT and the flood of new and complicated regulations. Retired teachers and nurses should be able to get relief work. Clubs need secretaries, local councils employ crossing wardens, shops can use extra help at the counter and in the storeroom at holiday time or periods of high pressure such as Christmas.

If you have nimble fingers and artistic talent you can make toys, costume jewellery, flower pictures and novelties for sale in local gift shops, or even in the large department stores. Another home 'industry' is acting as agent for a mail-order house. The strain of shopping in congested city centres is encouraging buying from catalogues, and women tend to be better than men at building up a mail-order agency.

Some people are natural salesmen and saleswomen, others shrivel up at the thought of selling the products of their brains and hands. If you are a shriveller, you had better seek an occupation that does not require personal confrontation with prospective customers. But first, you might try a little self-persuasion. Remember that there are timid customers as well as diffident sellers – you are a customer yourself. It is never too late to fight an inhibition.

For craftwork done at home you will need some basic equipment. Carpentry and metalwork require a bench and some good tools. Making up and repairing garments – one of the most widespread home occupations among women of all ages – has of course to be done on a sewing machine. There are more bedsitter and garden shed factories in Britain than the more affluent neighbours suspect.

The equipment is durable and the capital cost covered before long.

Materials are another matter. Building and decorating jobs may be costly to finance, and some customers are slow payers. You must not allow the business to get out of hand. After all, you want to enjoy your retirement, not exploit it to the verge of bankruptcy.

Beware of risking your savings in a shop. The illusion that retailing is easy dies hard. It can be a heart-breaking venture for the young. At sixty-plus it can be suicidal.

Enterprising types, in retirement as in their formative years, can find sources of income never tapped before. A recent radio broadcast featured two men who collected and sorted dumped cartons and other containers for sale to manufacturers. It was a kind of waste material that the more orthodox 'totters' had missed.

Not everyone is made of entrepreneurial material. You may prefer to be employed, no matter in how small a capacity. You have been warned that opportunities are sparse, but they do exist. Indeed prejudice against elderly people is diminishing. Employers are beginning to realize that cumulative experience is worth harnessing even if the service is rather slow. We knew a periodical publisher who employed three retired people as messengers. What they lacked in speed they made up in reliability. They were more loyal and much more courteous than the youths who had preceded them. And in spite of their advanced years, they lasted longer.

Retired people seeking employment find that their price and prestige have been devalued by age and circumstance. They will have to be prepared to accept a job of lower status and responsibility than the one they have retired from. Some will resent having to take instructions from people who so recently would have been their juniors. A hospital sister goes back as a nurse, a headmaster as an ordinary teacher. This is fair enough. The market determines labour values, and recognizes what has been lost by the age of sixty-five. If you find demotion intolerable, you should seek work of a different kind, in which you will not be haunted by past comparisons.

Some retired people feel guilty about augmenting their pensions with paid employment. They feel they are competing unfairly with the younger employed. Their conscience does them credit, but is misguided. The young and the old are rarely interchangeable on a job. Even when they are, both submit to the legitimate choices and chances of a competitive society. The right to work applies to people of all ages.

The young will always have the edge in the manpower market. If you are not self-employed, or have not had the kind of job that can be continued into retirement, you must expect difficulties and disappointments. All the more reason for planning well ahead.

Decide first what kind of work will suit your tastes and temperament. Should it be manual or clerical? making or selling? at home or away? on your own or with others? Whatever you choose it must be done well. There is no hope for a dabbler. Things are hard enough for the highly competent.

Next consideration is where to work. You should look for local possibilities. If you have to travel to the job the high cost of fares or petrol can cut deeply into the pay. And you have probably had enough travel on the old job.

THE ELDERLY ARE TEACHABLE

Third, how do you prepare for a new kind of job? You will probably need some training. You will also need to rid yourself of the 'old dogs/new tricks' complex. It is a myth that the elderly are unteachable. After all, there are many young pups who can't be taught any kind of tricks. Teachability varies with the individual. Many retired people tackle a new language or study a technical subject. There is no reason why they should not use the new knowledge for material profit.

If you want a refresher or up-dating course, or instruction in a new subject, you will probably be able to get it at an adult education centre. These centres are colleges of further education run by the local education authority. The syllabus is usually extensive and fees are moderate. Get particulars from your local library or direct from the college.

It is advisable to consult a member of the college staff before embarking on a course of study. He will ask about your general educational background, and how much you know about your chosen subject, so that he can make helpful recommendations. In these days of rapid change and technical advance, one can get out of date in a very short time. For instance, if your subject is accounts, you have to contend with a constant stream of new regulations. Even accountants in practice find it a strain to keep up.

Most of your fellow students will be young, but there may be one or two elders to keep you in countenance. You will have to accept the disparity. If there is an occasional snide remark from a brash youngster, deflect it with good humour.

The college may be able to tell you something about the possible employment follow-up to your study. But bear in mind that its function is to provide tuition, not to prepare you for or help you find a job.

As the number of employable pensioners grows, and their potential contribution to the nation's work is better understood, official provision may be made for developing this resource. There is as yet no special scheme on a national scale. In exceptional cases, the Government's Training Service Agency may be able to help. The Agency is responsible for TOPS (Training Opportunities Scheme) through which people over the age of nineteen can receive vocational training at a college of further education, a business school or a polytechnic, to help in improving their earning capacity or in changing employment.

There is no upward age limit. Middle-aged employees as well as the young have had reason to be grateful to TOPS. There is no bar to applications from people approaching or over retirement age, but the possibilities are fewer. Each application would be considered on its merits, depending on the type of work required, the area in which the applicant lived and the availability of work. Telephone the training officer at a Job Centre for an appointment – but keep your optimism under control.

Job Centres and the employment exchanges which they are gradually superseding, vary in their ability and willingness to help retired people seeking paid work. In times of high unemployment they are fully occupied with the needs of younger people. Opportunities are further limited by trade union rulings. For that reason alone senior citizens are more likely to find work in the service industries and the smaller firms where there is no closed shop than in large and highly unionized businesses.

There are a few private organizations specially concerned with the employment of older people. One of the best known is the Employment Fellowship. It has organized 140 work centres employing about 4000 elderly men and women on light work, such as packing, assembly and direct mail, for small and medium local firms. No less valuable than the pay is the companionship and the feeling of being usefully employed.

Smaller charitable groups have been formed in some localities to find work for pensioners. Ask your local Citizens' Advice Bureau whether there is one in your neighbourhood.

A recently established employment agency for retired people is Success After Sixty. From headquarters in 14 Great Castle Street,

London w1, and branches in Croydon, Slough, Watford and Manchester, it has persuaded and helped many employers to draw upon the retired people's pool for auxiliary staff. It is not a charity but a specialist commercial agency. Within its limited sphere of activity it has demonstrated that vacancies for odd jobs exist, that the people capable of filling them are available, and that both sides need to be brought together.

There is scope for more private (and indeed public) enterprises of this kind. As the number of pensioners increases, the national burden of supplementary benefits will force the issue of providing paid work for retired people.

The Institute of Directors has a Retirement Advisory Bureau one of whose purposes is to help members to find employment in retirement. A few years ago the jobs sought were mainly voluntary, now they are mainly paid – a sign of the times which needs no comment. Much of the employment is short-term consultancy for small firms and for charities. The early retired (say at fifty-five) may get full time jobs at home or overseas.

Whether or not there is any organized employment aid in your area, you will still search the vacancies columns in your local newspaper and the 'wants' notices in your newsagent's windows. Be cautious in your response. Make sure that you are not likely to be exploited by employers of cut price labour. Elderly people on the fringe of employment will not expect the same rates as younger full-time employees, but they should get a reasonable return for their work.

Look around you for opportunities nearby. The branch library may want a stop-gap at holiday time. A newly opened supermarket may need a relief cashier, or help in filling shelves and attaching price tabs to packages. A new estate agent may want clerical or telephone services. An insurance broker, an architect or an advertising agent in the new office block may have an opening for your kind of talent.

An additional source is the grapevine. People hear of jobs and are glad to pass on the information. They will not tell you unless they know you want work. Therefore let your friends and neighbours know that you are in the market.

We have warned you that employment possibilities for retired people are restricted and elusive, the market largely unorganized, the attitude rather discouraging and often hostile. Nevertheless, as we have said, the proportion of pensioners still earning is impressive

Initiative is evidently not lacking despite the infliction of advancing years.

Whether you gain financially from a job depends upon your age and the size of your earnings. The anomaly has been discussed in Part Three of this book. As you know, if you are between sixty-five and seventy (sixty and sixty-five for women), your pension is subject to the earnings rule. That is, for every pound you earn over a certain amount, the government will dock your retirement pension. You may have so little left that job satisfaction will have to be the sole reward. To be worth-while the pay will have to be enough to leave a useful surplus over and above the obliterated pension. Or, if circumstances permit, you might decide to remain in full-time employment and defer claiming the pension till you turn seventy, when it will be increased by a small amount in recognition of your self-restraint.

There is one way in which you can employ yourself (not the same thing as self-employment): you may not have had time when you were in a job to do your own house painting, repairs and maintenance. In retirement you have the leisure (and, we hope, the skill) to do it yourself. You can regard the saving in labour cost as an indirect addition to income.

9

Serving the Community

We said that about half of the newly retired people have some paid work. Looked at another way this means that half do not. Why not? What do they do with their time, and what guides their choice?

There are a very few who do not need the money. They have adequate investment income and substantial, perhaps index-linked, pensions. They can still use extra money, but they can afford to spend their time on preferred unpaid occupations.

A rather more numerous class, though less affluent, are still in no urgent need. They feel that forty or fifty years of working for a living are enough. The time has come for living without working. No one can blame them. We hope they will enjoy their emancipation.

Some want paid work but fail to find it. We offered suggestions in the last chapter, but pointed out that opportunities were limited. The limitations are sometimes in the person and his experience. His work had been highly specialized and non-transferable. He is not resourceful in making money out of his interests. But life in retirement, we hope, provides compensations.

Many retired people, whether or not in part-time paid work, give some of their leisure to voluntary causes. They have much to offer. They have fought a lifetime's battles and gained experience and understanding. Though less energetic than the young and middle-aged, they have fewer distractions. Retirement enables them to expand an existing activity, or take up a long cherished cause which had been crowded out by the urgency of earning a living.

Charitable work is satisfying in many ways. It provides an outlet for pure compassion through relieving distress of body and mind. It permits fulfilment of a sense of mission. It presents a comforting contrast between the giver and the receiver of benefits. It enables managerial types to take charge of effort and people. All motives are mixed, but one must beware of confusing 'do-gooders' with people who, for whatever combination of reasons, do genuine and unadulterated good.

The scope for alleviation of suffering and the support of socially desirable causes is vast in any society. There is never enough help in manpower or money. The welfare state does not, and cannot be expected to, provide completely for all charitable needs. Private endeavour is still strong in Britain. Not all the worthy causes are charities in the generally accepted or the wider statutory sense of the term. Opinions differ on the value of many causes which are listed as charities. But people have the right to spend money and energy on pet schemes, however eccentric they may seem to most of us. Retirement is a release mechanism for support, promotion, prevention or suppression of many things you have at heart or on your mind.

Since charities are almost invariably poor, they can pay for only the minimum of help. There are some essential full-time professional services – legal, financial and administrative – which have to be paid for. There are others which are not remunerated, but involve the helpers in expenses which they cannot be expected to pay out of their own pockets. But there is a great deal of part-time and temporary work which requires the expenditure only of time, ability and goodwill. Many retired people have an abundance of all three.

Beware of plunging into voluntary work with more enthusiasm than discretion. You and the cause will both suffer. Even in the most needy causes, fanaticism can be a menace. Decide what you can contribute in expertise and time. What you provide should be as good in quality as paid services – and better than some. Only the best is good enough for charity. Inadequate or half-hearted effort is morally wrong and damages the cause. A voluntary organization cannot easily exert the same discipline as an employer. The helper must supply his own discipline.

Don't over-estimate the amount of time you can spare. If you do, and then have to default, you will cause more trouble than if you had not started. You owe some time to yourself and your friends. Leave yourself enough leisure for the less earnest, less unselfish occupations, which are among the legitimate perquisites of retirement. Time may not be money to the fully retired but it has a value. It is a mistake to give more of it than you can afford.

Do you get on well with people?

Which would you find most convenient: to give a fixed number of days a week or a month? To work every other day or week? To work on the premises or in your own time at home? To be on call for relief work or sudden contingency? Choose your cause and ask what is wanted. It helps both sides if you have a provisional pattern of service in mind.

Next, ask yourself the same questions as our hypothetical retirement planner. Do you get on well with people or are you a loner? Are you a desk or a field worker? Do you like routine or change? Do you want to be an officer or a ranker?

The question of leadership is a delicate one. There may be an established hierarchy in the organization you want to join, and they will resent the intrusion of a new prospective boss. The personal strains in commerce and industry are slight compared with the conflicts in some voluntary organizations. Volunteers resent being pushed around. Even if you enter as a boss, you will have to tread carefully. Leadership requires tact as well as organizing ability.

There are therefore deeper questions you will have to ask yourself. Are you diplomatic or heavy-handed, liked or feared, dominant or yielding, patient or impatient, quick-tempered or controlled? The answers will not constitute a moral judgement. You will be conducting a recruitment interview, only the interviewer and the interviewee will be the same person. The report on this dual personality will tell you what kind of job to aim at, and what to avoid.

Even if you are a leader type, you will find that you cannot lead everywhere or all the time. If you join an organization as a volunteer you should approach it with the same humility, or philosophy, as you would a paid job, whether full-time at the peak of your career or part-time after you have retired. In other words, you must be prepared to take orders. Otherwise, of course, keep out. The work may be humbler than you have been accustomed to, but it may still be needed and important.

Even modest unpaid jobs may not be as easily procurable as you might expect. It is true that charities and other causes are urgently in need of volunteers. But they are not undiscriminating. They have to be selective in the interests of those who are dependent upon them. The gift horse has to be sound in wind and limb. Just as the cause or its organization may not be what you want, so the converse must also apply.

Ideally, the volunteer should be responsible, equable, intelligent, co-operative, without personal ambition, 'all passion spent'. The full specification is rare, but an approximation will do.

KINDS OF CHARITY WORK

Voluntary work is so varied and there is so much interlocking and overlapping of organizations that classification is almost impossible. Some attempt should however be made if you want to find your way around and choose a landing place.

The group of activities that comes most immediately to mind is care for those in greatest need. It is concerned with the poor, the old, the sick, the handicapped and the victimized. It tries to relieve loneliness, procure money or goods for those whom society has overlooked, bring comfort to invalids in hospital or at home, look after neglected children, battered wives and other victims of criminal assault.

You can help them either directly or, preferably, via one of the established charities. In pre-welfare state days it was the poor who helped the poor. Nobody else did. Today it seems equally appropriate for the old to help their less fortunate contemporaries. You can visit the old, the disabled, the blind, the housebound sick; shop for them, read to them, change their library books and, if you drive, take them to their club or to the clinic for treatment, or deliver 'meals-on-wheels'.

You can join your local hospital's League of Friends. Some hospitals have a welfare official to organize voluntary services. These include visiting, escorting, helping in the out-patie'nts canteen, taking the telephone trolley to the bedside.

Some of the old and incapacitated need nothing more than companionship. Loneliness is a killer, but first it injures the mind. A person living alone and cut off from contact with others by infirmity needs someone to talk to, someone who can report what is happening in the inaccessible world outside.

All these services should be, as far as possible, undertaken regularly. The recipients look forward to them and should be spared disappointment. In addition to regularity, they demand patience and understanding. Invalids and cripples can be peevish with good cause, the very old can be crotchety, and those verging on senility difficult to cope with. If saintliness proves a strain, be sensible and leave the more trying jobs to the born saints.

Again, if you shrink from contact with illness, senility and physical infirmity, don't reproach yourself. We don't all have to be Albert Schweitzers and Florence Nightingales. There is enough variety in voluntary work to suit all temperaments. Those who minister to the sick would probably hate the equally important clerical and administrative services that you would undertake cheerfully.

Charitable societies, youth clubs, and clubs for the elderly need appeals organizers, committee members, fund raisers, clothes collectors, helpers at jumble sales, treasurers, typists, envelope addressers, telephonists, producers and deliverers of publicity material. Fund-raising may involve knocking on doors for contributions. It will make friends and enemies for you. Most people are either naturally charitable or ashamed to say no, but some are mean and a few offensive. Sensitive helpers should stick to the desk work.

Church and mission work attract volunteers in spite of complaints about the decline of religion in our society. Some of the work is gentle and humble, like cleaning the church brasses. Some is sterner stuff, such as prison visiting, liaison with prisoners' families, helping discharged prisoners via the specialized societies. Rescue work with the Samaritans can be harrowing but also morally rewarding.

Teaching and communication offer scope for people with specialized training and experience. If you have been a teacher or a technician, gained proficiency in a foreign language, artwork, acting, stage production or music, you will find eager learners at local clubs and specialized societies. If you have travelled widely, or studied local history or antiquities, you will probably get an enthusiastic audience

D

at the Women's Institute or the Townswomen's Guild or a Senior Citizens' Club.

An associated service is helping people to understand and complete forms. We all suffer from the jargon and convoluted instructions of the bureaucracy. Few except accountants and football pool addicts can navigate the documents successfully. The old and the ignorant are bewildered and frightened. They will bless you if you can help them to fill the forms and if you can act as spokesman before authority.

It should not be necessary but may be advisable to remind you that the word spokesman and other verbal masculinities are bisexual in the context of this book. In many spheres women voluntary workers predominate. Apart from specifically masculine and feminine problems usually vocational or domestic, women and men can be equally effective.

Both sexes provide active political partisans. Local party organizations depend very much on volunteers. Debates, canvassing, circularizing, fund-raising through 'bring and buy' sales, dances and other entertainments, are year-round activities increasing in tempo at election-time. As you might expect, senior citizens tend to gravitate to the less extreme causes and non-party controversies.

Many such causes are social and only incidentally political if, for instance, the villain is the local council. You may like to write to the newspapers and participate in petitions to the offending authority at local or national level. You can support your ratepayers' association, consumer interests, the preservation of rights of way; fight for better lighting, for protection of pedestrians at dangerous crossings and junctions, for and against fluoridation of the local water supply. The war against despoilers of the environment is intensifying. Protests against rubbish dumping and pollution, demands for the cleaning up of eyesores, are exciting and worthy activities for people with spare time and an articulate conscience.

Voluntary work for causes, whether charitable, political, or un-classifiable, is usually a corporate effort. There are however some people who act on their own. We know men and women who seek out housebound and overburdened people in their vicinity, do their shopping, take their young children to school, advise them on their rights and argue their case with officialdom. Some of these self-contained benefactors include animals among their protégés, and take charge of abandoned cats and dogs.

WHERE TO APPLY

If you prefer to work with others, where do you find them? Look first at your local newspaper. It reports whatever makes news in the area, however trivial from the general point of view. There you will learn who talked about what at the Women's Institutes in half a dozen villages. You will probably find that there is an old people's welfare council, a society for mentally handicapped children, branches of the Salvation Army, the British Legion, and the Bible Society. The League of Hospital Friends may have held a fair to raise funds for providing wards with radio. There will be fund-raising committees for research into such mysterious diseases as multiple sclerosis and cystic fibrosis. Decisions and doings of the local council's social services committee will be featured.

All those organizations use voluntary services and need yet more. Call upon any that interest you, including the Social Services Department at the town hall. Enquire what they want, tell them what you can do.

Your library should be able to help you to add to the list. The reference department will either have or be able to obtain for you the *Charities Digest*, published annually by the Family Welfare Association, and the *Voluntary Social Services Directory and Handbook*, published by the National Council of Social Service, the co-ordinating body for voluntary social effort. They give enough information in most cases on which to base further enquiries.

For further enquiries, especially about the local situation, go to the Citizens' Advice Bureau in your district. In fact, you might be wise to consult them in the first instance. The CAB is the country's great clearing-house for information. If it can't answer your question, it will find out who can. Each local bureau keeps informed of events and changing conditions in its territory. Once a month it receives updated information from the national headquarters on new legislation and changes in government provisions affecting the citizen. It is a source of help on personal and family problems, health, tenancy and consumer worries. It is an obvious source of information for prospective voluntary workers seeking an outlet.

The CAB itself is staffed mainly by volunteers. It may be able to use your services – if they are good enough. Its standards are exacting. It needs trained people and is willing to train promising recruits. One of the secrets of the CAB's success is that it contrives to call a highly professional tune whether or not it pays the piper.

Another organization with a fine reputation which offers help and relies on help is the Women's Royal Voluntary Service. This too is widely represented throughout the country. Its charity is all-embracing. It includes homes, clubs, meals-on-wheels and companionship for the old and infirm, health care and holidays for mothers and babies, trolley shops in hospitals, assistance for refugees and victims of disaster.

In spite of its name the WRVS is not staffed by women only. It offered scope for male volunteers long before the sex equality legislation breached ancient sanctuaries in both camps.

Age Concern, as its name implies, is more specialized. This too is a nationwide organization co-ordinating local welfare efforts and co-operating with central and local government in providing for the needs of the elderly. It organizes luncheon clubs, holidays, transport, and friendly visiting, and trains voluntary workers for the care of old people. Some of the local organizations under the Age Concern umbrella have different names. If you cannot find them in the telephone directory or the local newspaper ask the social service department or the CAB.

Most voluntary service is charitable. It need not be so. No one would consider a constituency political party organization as a charity. There is however a common factor. Voluntary work is something you do for others without pay. There may of course be a moral or intellectual pay-off; even party politics can inspire a sense of mission.

The next chapter will discuss the things you do neither for pay nor voluntarily for others, but for your own enjoyment. The activities in the first two categories may be no less enjoyable, but they differ in purpose, if not wholly in kind, from those in the third.

10

In Your Own Time

Unless you choose to fill your retirement with paid and/or voluntary work, you will have time you can call your own. What will you do with it?

The choice of activity is vast. The advantage over doing paid and voluntary work is that you have a free hand. You will study your aptitudes, experience and inclinations (look again at the pre-retirement plan in Part One) and follow their guidance. Few people are so limited as to lack or be incapable of developing an interest.

Your immediate action station is your home. We spend our lives in two environments. One is home and family. The other is the outside world. The workplace constitutes a very large part of that outer environment. When we retire from full-time employment, home looms larger for most of us than the world outside. Retirement is a kind of home-coming.

Let us assume that all the possible domestic conflicts that might arise out of retirement have been resolved. Your wife's fear that you would be in her way has proved groundless. You don't moon around the house like a lost soul. You are shaved and dressed in time for breakfast. You don't fancy yourself as a chef, and keep away from the kitchen till wanted for carving or breaking up hard frozen foods. What now?

There are jobs in the house that you have saved for retirement – woodwork to be painted, walls to be papered, a door to be re-hung, tiles to be grouted and, if you have the skill, cupboards to be made and fitted. Here is a new possibility of domestic conflict. If your work is not good enough, don't do it yourself. Your wife wants the house to look smarter, not shoddier. And don't imagine you have 'all the time in the world' and let the painting drag on for weeks. The workman may be in his element, but his mate hates the mess.

Jobs in the house are not a continuing occupation. When the arrears have been cleared up you can sit back or turn to other things – till the paint starts flaking again. There are rare exceptions. One we know of is a household where the husband's skill and patience are infinite and the wife's appetite for change in her surroundings is inexhaustible. They live in a constant turmoil of reconstruction and both are happy.

If you are not a handyman of all trades, don't tinker with the danger points in the house. There have been cases of amateur gas fitters and electricians who have had a shorter retirement than nature intended.

SOCIAL LIFE EXPANDS

Retirement provides more time for social life. It does at the same time reduce the money available for social enjoyment. But retired people are usually old enough to be moderate in their indulgences. You can see your friends more often, particularly if they too are retired. Life can expand, instead of shrink, in retirement.

It can expand for both partners. Husband and wife can have more time together, visiting friends, taking excursions as far as funds permit, playing bridge, going to shows and concerts. Some couples like to balance their joint interests with a few exclusive ones. If your wife likes an occasional party with her friends, the gathering may be less inhibited without you. Your wife may have other social outlets in the Women's Institute or the Townswomen's Guild. A life of one's own and a life together are not incompatible, and in some households are positively beneficial.

Women are often more 'clubbable' than men. Most localities have an old people's club, under such names as Senior Citizens' Club and – more sentimentally – Evergreen or Darby and Joan Club. There are usually many more Joans than Darbies. The clubs vary in what they provide. There is always a comfortable chair and a cup of tea or coffee and a cake at very much below the economic price. Some provide lunches, radio and television, and organize entertainments and outings.

Those clubs are a godsend to lonely people whose tastes and means are modest, and whose social life and mobility are restricted. They offer companionship, common interests and sympathy in shared disabilities. But they do not suit everyone. They lack the variety and stimulus of a mixed gathering.

You may prefer a less restrictive club with a wider range in membership and amenities. Indeed, you may have belonged to a club long before retirement. There are, in addition, societies for every kind of human interest, from archaeology to zoology and from debating to philately. Some of the societies offer other than social and avocational benefits; for instance, the economy of bulk-buying and of party travel.

Travel, when you like and for as long as you like, can be one of the joys of retirement. The joy and the opportunities are curbed for most people by the cost of public and private transport and accommodation. You can however take advantage of mid-week and out-of-season reductions, and rail concessions and club schemes for senior citizens. Coach trips are usually cheaper than rail. Exchange arrangements may be worth while, if you can bear the thought of someone else taking over your house.

Cost is not the only, and not always the main, consideration. Long coach journeys can be too tiring for elderly people. A cheap package holiday abroad may be procured at too much sacrifice of comfort and good food. An out-of-season holiday may be cold and wet. If you can't afford the best every time, you may find that leisure is the only holiday component you have in plenty.

You must expect to take less active holidays as you get older. If you still run a car and enjoy touring from place to place don't overdo the daily mileage and the sight-seeing. Try more day trips over short distances, either by car or using concession tickets for senior citizens on local transport. Exploring the home ground can be a novel and exciting experience.

The young and the not so young with energy and a regular pay packet are no doubt wise to take holidays far afield. But there are antiquities, museums, art galleries and beauty spots within fairly easy and inexpensive reach of most areas. Age has a chance to pick up what youth has missed.

Your interest in the locality can be as deep as you wish to make it. You can track down published historical and topographical material with the help of your library, search parish records, and compile your own local history. Whether it is publishable or not, it makes you something of an authority. You will be listened to with interest and no little respect in your neighbourhood.

Studying local history and topography is both an outdoor and an indoor activity. Most leisure occupations fall mainly into one of these two divisions. The supreme outdoor attraction, especially in retirement, is gardening. There is no need to tell a dedicated gardener how varied and absorbing a garden can be. It might be rewarding to tell a non-gardener: he could be open to conversion.

If you are an experienced gardener you will know how to limit your ambition. A garden can become a tyranny if it demands more work than your strength or other interests warrant. Some take on an allotment in addition to the back garden and enjoy the labour and the produce. A convert to gardening or a potterer who is becoming keen needs to plan his garden to fit comfortably into his total programme. A knowledgeable friend or neighbour will be glad to advise.

Gardening, like exploring the neighbourhood, can be as learned or as simple as you choose. You do not need to know the Latin names. But you do need to know what you are doing and why. You can aim to grow a prize marrow or a glamorous chrysanthemum for your local show, or make an attractive floral display to enjoy from a deck chair.

There is a social aspect to gardening even if you don't join a society. You can share know-how and cuttings with a neighbour and lament together the deficiences of your soil compared with the prolific patch on the other side of the fence. Weeds and insect pests are an inexhaustible topic in themselves.

We spoke about sport in a chapter on health, but its therapeutic value is incidental. No one except a faddist plays football or tennis as a medical treatment. Outdoor sports will be less strenuous and less competitive as one grows older. But medical science and the layman's increased understanding of healthy living have prolonged vigour in both sexes to a degree that would have been unbelievable a generation ago. Though people over sixty don't play rugger or hockey, many of them still play golf, go swimming and dancing with benefit and not injury to health. A retired acquaintance in his sixties, who golfs and gardens with undiminished zest after suffering a coronary and losing a kidney in his fifties, is an object of admiration but not of wonder.

As we pointed out earlier it is those who take no exercise who are at risk. There are indoor games – table tennis, billiards, badminton – which provide in varying degrees stimulus for body and brain.

Angling continues to be a popular outdoor activity, without any natural age limit. It will grow as our polluted rivers are restored to health and restocked. It is a restful and often a solitary interest, but it can be enjoyed in company and, for the true devotee, competitively. There are specialized periodicals for those who are interested in angling as a subject. In fact, there is hardly a sport or craft or hobby which is not covered by at least one journal. You will find them in a directory of newspapers and magazines at your reference library.

Bird watching

Bird-watching is another growing and very satisfying occupation. Like gardening it can be as scientific as you wish to make it. You can watch for hours from a hide as a serious student of ornithology, or satisfy a less technical curiosity from a window facing your garden. Hang a bird-house from a tree and put out food and water to entice visitors. They will soon acquire confidence. You will be entertained to discover how they differ in habits and character within the same species. Every bird is an individual. Experienced watchers can distinguish one sparrow from another by its shape and markings.

HOBBIES AND CRAFTS

We have tried, without complete success, to avoid the word hobby for the spare-time occupations that are neither remunerative nor charitable but just beguiling. It has a juvenile implication. It suggests collecting matchbox tops and plaiting corn dollies. Not that these occupations are contemptible. Corn dollies are an ancient fertility symbol studied by anthropologists. And a display of matchboxes in hundreds is colourful, ingenious and amusing. There is nothing collectable that can't find a serious collector.

Postage stamps are among the most widely collected items. They offer much more scope and subtlety of interest than non-collectors realize. You can specialize in the stamps of a single country, or in pictorials, or in first day 'covers' (i.e. stamped envelopes cancelled on the day of issue). You can look out for variations in printing and perforations, or errors, omissions and other oddities. These add to the value of the collection as an investment. A collector is not simply a magpie.

Collecting is increasing. Junk shops and antique markets are springing up everywhere. Coins, first editions and prints can be expensive, but bargains can still be found off the connoisseur's track. Yesterday's throw-outs are becoming collectors' items alongside the day-before-yesterday's artifacts. Old catalogues, showcards, toys, bottles, labels and tin cans are being rescued from refuse dumps. Store them where they won't offend a tidy housewife. Shells and pebbles are beautiful and less extravagant in cost and space. Flotsam and jetsam eroded by the waves can be decorative in a bizarre way.

If you have a hobby (sorry – there seems to be no other word), be thorough and methodical. Expertise is part of the satisfaction. Learn something about the history of postage stamps, the geology of pebbles, the processes involved in printed matter, the artistry of old keys and watch hands, the social background of samplers, old scrap books or whatever you choose. The same applies to anything you fashion or concoct.

Wine, for instance. There is a vogue for wine-making. Some of the products are nauseating to everyone except the vintner. Continue to experiment till you have made something rather better than commercial plonk. It is possible to make a palatable alcoholic drink out of almost any fruit or vegetable.

It is not impossible to learn a new craft after retirement, especially if you already have some manual skill. Most craft work starts much earlier in life, but retirement provides leisure for expansion. You may already have the necessary tools and a spare room or shed where you can operate undisturbed. If you have never worked with your hands but have an urge to make things, you might find the necessary tuition at your local college.

The list of possible subjects would fill pages. They include leather-work and carving, model-making in wood or metal, pottery, up-holstery, photography, cookery and confectionery, gold and silver-work (if you can afford the materials), costume jewellery, lampshades, rugs, paper sculpture and mobiles – any utility or luxury for the house or the person. Whatever subject you choose, you will probably find that there is a society at no great distance where you can meet fellow workers and talk shop. In spite of the steeply rising cost of books, craft manuals can still be bought at reasonable prices. Your library will have the more advanced and expensive ones, or will borrow them for you from other libraries.

Some women's crafts are a normal part of housekeeping. Those who can't wield some kind of needle are a small minority. But craft needlework is in a different class. Many Women's Institutes hold classes. The work ranges in skill from simple knitting and patchwork to lace-making, embroidery and tapestry.

There is no sharp division between arts and crafts. The most accomplished craftsmen are also artists. Some of the skills, in music and painting for instance, are more difficult to acquire in one's later years. There have been cases of elderly people learning to paint or to play an instrument with distinction, but they have been exceptional enough to go on record. There is nothing to stop you from having a go. You may not make the halls or the galleries, but you may become good enough to liven up a party.

Writing, which might seem to be the easiest of the arts since we all use words, is in practice one of the most difficult to acquire. Even articulate people become paralysed at the sight of blank paper. But you need not write with publication in view or even for private circulation. You could start a diary. A small minority of people are addicted diarists, but most lives go unrecorded. Write down, without straining after elegant composition, things seen, heard, thought about, or remembered. You will fill volumes. Then bind the volumes in attractive boards (book-binding is a pleasant craft in itself).

Re-reading one's old diaries after many years is an absorbing experience – and sometimes a revelation. You might graduate to an autobiography. We have met a retired army officer who, on the verge of eighty and having never composed anything more creative than a letter, wrote down his war experience and had it privately printed and bound for his family and friends.

We must not forget those almost universal media of indoor

recreation, radio and television. Like books they are a multiple source of entertainment and instruction. They bring you sport, laughter and excitement, music and drama, history, geography and science. You can use radio and television as a relaxation or a soporific; or you can be selective and base further study on the subjects chosen.

Radio, television and a record player are more than luxuries to the elderly retired. When cost, weather or infirmity restrict your concert- and theatre-going and attendance at spectator sports, you can still enjoy a performance by the world's greatest exponents. But unless you are housebound you should contrive occasionally to see a live per- formance. One can get too mechanized, too detached from the crowd.

Inevitably, one becomes more of a spectator and less of a participant in old age. To the vigilant the world provides spectacles in plenty. At holiday camps you will see a few people who are much too old for the standard fun and games, yet sit happily outside their 'chalets' day after day. They enjoy the noise and movement. They like to see young people having a good time.

For some people, the supreme benefit that retirement brings is more time for reading. They are usually the systematic readers, who read for intellectual profit as well as pleasure. They may be lifelong students, adding endlessly to their knowledge of a favourite subject. Those with adventurous minds embark on new subjects. An inde- fatigable woman we heard of was an accumulator of languages. At well past seventy she was adding Chinese to her repertoire.

No one is too old to join a college of further education or a poly- technic. Some mature students have fulfilled an old and thwarted ambition to get a degree. You have to have the appropriate basic qualification, but this too can be acquired by study.

The Open University has raised the hopes and fulfilled the dreams of thousands. It teaches mainly by correspondence supplemented with special television and radio programmes. A course takes longer than at a residential university, but the quality is comparable and the cost much lower. Write for prospectuses and advice to The Open University, PO Box 48, Milton Keynes, Bucks.

As we have tried to show, retirement opens up vast possibilities for enjoying leisure. This chapter presents a sample only. Nevertheless, there are people who start retirement without anything to replace their former occupation. They say, 'I've no ability or interests outside the old job. I've never had a hobby. How can I start one?'

A hobby can't be prescribed, nor an interest be imposed from outside.

One has to make an effort, look around and ask around for subjects, note what a friend or acquaintance is doing, give it a trial, drop it if it doesn't work and try something else. Just as appetite comes with eating so interest can come with experiment. If everything else fails, thank technology for television.

II

Home or Away? – Pros and Cons of Moving

Where will you live when you retire? Having broken with the past in one respect, will you complete the break by moving away? If so, moving where? To a smaller house, bungalow, flat in the same district? Or to another part of the country? Or even overseas?

That thought comes to everyone planning or approaching retirement. The great majority decide to stay where they are. For some of the others the decision is the most difficult that they have had to face. You will remember that our hypothetical planner left it open. There were things he could not foresee so far ahead.

How can you know, when you start planning in your fifties, whether the house will be suitable ten, fifteen, twenty years on? You may make a bad move and find that it is irreversible. Or you may postpone the move till it is too late to cope with the cost or the fatigue.

Cost is a major consideration in any case. Many problems besides the financial one depend upon the kind of tenure; whether you own or rent the house, what size it is, whether it is a council house, a flat in a large block, or a shared apartment. They depend also upon the kind of person you are.

People are either movers or stayers. Some have made a dozen moves or more and enjoyed the excitement of change. Others are like cats, attached to old haunts and restless in a new environment. The psychology of domicile must have a place in the decision.

There are problems if you want to move, but many more if you *need* to move. A compelling factor will be the size of accommodation. Oversize is not revealed suddenly at the moment of retirement. The house was too big for your needs when the children left home. But on retirement it will probably be bigger than you can afford. You will have to consider whether you can economize by moving, and if not, whether other reasons must take priority over economy.

Excessive room can be a burden. Unused space has still to be kept clean and maintained to prevent deterioration. If you have no domestic help and do your own decoration the work will get beyond your strength in time. That may be true also of the garden. What was a recreation up to your sixties may become a losing battle after seventy. So you begin to plan a move into smaller accommodation.

You may not have realized, even when you made an inventory for insurance, how many objects you have accumulated by purchase and gift. Will you take them with you into half the number of rooms? It will be like living in a warehouse. Can you bear to part with any of them? Which will you keep and what will you do with the rest? Sell the best, perhaps for less than they are worth? Throw out unsaleable trivia, oozing with sentimental associations? Surrender treasured possessions to the jumble collectors who have been pestering you for years?

There are other snags in moving to a smaller place. Changes, repairs and redecoration will be costly. Carpets and curtains may not fit. What you have saved in the end may not be worth the upheaval. This does not mean that you should decide against a move. It does mean however that you should plan carefully, listing all the obstacles and how to overcome them, or why to accept them. The decision is too important to be hurried.

As part of your plan you will have considered the practicality of sharing your house or dividing it and letting a portion. Dividing, if feasible, involves capital outlay and a hope that you will recover it before many years. Sharing, or what amounts to the same thing, taking a lodger, might disrupt your life more than you would want to risk.

Let us suppose therefore that you will look for smaller accommodation in your neighbourhood. You will want a place that is easy to run, with a small garden or a patio with space for tubs. You may prefer a bungalow, in anticipation of a time when stairs could be difficult. Or you may choose a flat in a block, so long as you are sure that you will not miss the garden, or mind the proximity of neighbours above and below you as well as on either side.

Those considerations apply whether you want to buy or rent other accommodation. In either case, you may be helped or thwarted by the state of the market. As this is being written, the law favours tenants against landlords, and many owners are reluctant to let. But legislation changes, and anything we said about it could be out of date and misleading by the time this book appeared. We shall keep to generalities, underlined with a caution to get expert advice before committing yourself to a move. If you have owned a property you will know some of the pitfalls. There are many more today, both for owners and tenants.

The problems multiply if you move some distance away. You will have to take account of what you are leaving behind, and whether the sacrifice is worth-while; and what you are going to, and whether you will be happy there.

Over the years you have acquired social and emotional vested interests in your locality. You are on good terms with the neighbours and have friends within easy visiting distance. The shopping is adequate; the services – bank, hairdresser, doctor, dentist – accessible and long standing; social and religious affiliations mature and cordial. This is your home ground. You have taken root.

Now you have the retirement itch, to start your new life in new surroundings. It is the same kind of impulse that drives younger people to Australia. But you must be aware of the difference. Old roots are not so easy to transplant, and young lives have career potential. The young can make new contacts; the old need to cling to those they have. Think hard and weigh the consequences before you move. Otherwise, as with marrying in haste, you will repent at leisure.

EXPLORE BEFORE YOU MOVE

Explore the locality you have in mind and make searching enquiries. Will the climate suit you, or is it bleak, wet and windy? Is the place too hilly for comfortable walking? How good is the public transport? Does the place have the familiar amenities – theatre, concerts, library, clubs? Is the shopping expensive? If you have a paid but non-transferable job, will you be able to get a replacement? Is the local council negligent or extravagant? If you are quitting a council house and hoping for a transfer, will you get it? You will have to become reconciled, for a time at least, to a feeling of exile and loneliness. Is the place too far for your friends to drop in? Are you a faithful correspondent? Will estrangement worry you? Do you make new friends easily? List the pros and cons, measuring your characteristics against those of the location, and act upon a judicious assessment.

Not least, look into the reasons for your choice. Then ask yourself whether they are sound; whether, that is, you would approve of them in someone else.

The reasons may be nostalgic, sentimental, superficial — and irrational. You may have known the place as a child and have hankered after the golden dream. Psychologists would call it a back-to-the-womb complex and advise you to resist it. Or you may have spent a glorious holiday there, illumined in your memory by a golden girl. Or the attraction may be even slighter than that; a place you have heard about or glimpsed in passing. A calculating look at such places with an ageing eye will probably shatter the dream, and sweep the pieces out of your system.

Some hankerings have a deeper fixation. People who have lived in a large town all their lives often develop illusions about village life. It looks so happy and peaceful, sheltered from the rat race, and perhaps bypassed by the motorway. To crown all, housing is cheap.

Before plunging into paradise and landing on the fringe of purgatory, ask people who have lived in a village for a faithful report. Some villagers resent urban immigrants who force up house rents and prices. Even in a tolerant atmosphere, one might chafe against the lack of the familiar amenities, and be bored by the local pleasures.

On the other hand, you may have the right temperament for country life. We know a strikingly successful case. Husband and wife, lifelong London dwellers, both retired from jobs in the city centre, bought a cottage in a village in one of our more in-grown counties. They grow vegetables, bottle fruit, and participate in local life and politics.

Those two happy rusticators have a car. Without one's own transport village life for an ex-town dweller can become intolerable. Do you drive? Will you continue to run a car? The answers to those questions may be decisive for the most ardent country lover.

Even stronger than the call of the country is the lure of the sea. The view can be just as deceptive. We see it in holiday colours under a summer sky. It is difficult to imagine how lifeless and bleak it can be in winter. Large numbers of people do retire to the coast. Some resorts seem to be pensioner colonies. The dwellers obviously enjoy the company of their own kind and the boisterous invasion in the season. No doubt they have also come to terms with friends and relatives seeking free board and lodging at holiday times.

Seaside resorts with a large proportion of pensioners have a special problem. The welfare facilities, health especially, tend to become overloaded. You should include that possibility among your preliminary enquiries.

Before burning your boats at a seaside resort or a village, visit the place at various seasons and stay long enough to get a fair impression. As Kipling said of the ladies, 'You never can tell till you've tried 'em!'.

Sheltered from the rat race

The attraction of the environment is in some cases of minor importance. The reason for moving is to be near the married children. 'Now we have time,' runs the argument, 'we can see more of them and the grandchildren.' Are you sure you will be welcome? Even closely knit families can be too close for comfort. Since absence makes the heart grow fonder, the converse is worth pondering before you invade the younger generation's territory.

Of course, there are cases where it works out very happily. A widowed (non-interfering) mother has her own room in a married daughter's house and as far as possible lives her own life. Or the parents share the house with the young couple by a business-like arrangement. But both sides must discuss and dispose of all the snags at the start. And there must be an escape clause, without recriminations, for both sides.

PROBLEMS OF EMIGRATING

In the days, not very distant, when living was cheaper on the Continent than in Britain, some retired people took advantage of their new freedom to settle abroad. Today the prospect is, financially, less enticing. The more obvious difficulties remain — language, food, customs, politics and the lonely feeling of being an alien. Even the weather may turn out to be no better than at home. Some voluntary exiles are happy enough; witness the established expatriate colonies in Spain and Italy. But one hears less of the failures.

Don't be led astray by comparisons of income. Taxation may be lower and net income much higher than in Britain, but the gains must be weighed against the cost of living. One must remember also that conditions which favour the native wage earner may bear heavily on a retired foreigner's fixed income. If on careful reflection you do decide to emigrate, keep an escape route open to the home country.

If you are married, you will want your wife to agree on any decision to move or not to move. People who live alone have no conflicts except those of indecision. If you have a rented apartment and few belongings, you can go where you like and retreat if it doesn't work. You will still be subject to the vagaries of the market and impeded by financial limitations. Most of what we have said applies no matter how free you are to move around.

We may seem to have painted too gloomy a picture of moving. The purpose was not dissuasion but a warning against illusion. New horizons can be stimulating, but you must know what they hold in store. If all you have liked about your home district has been the accessibility of your work place, you may gain more than you lose by moving. But any move should be thought out as realistically and as logically as the other elements in your pre-retirement planning.

This is in fact the tail-piece to your personal audit. Like the rest of the plan it will be clearer if you put it on paper. Its purpose is to balance the pros and cons of every possibility and achieve a common-sense solution. What follows is a specimen scheme, which you can modify and enlarge to fit your circumstances.

PROS AND CONS OF STAYING

1   *Advantages of house and location*
Comfortable house. We have given it a character. Mortgage term nearing completion. A good property, bound to appreciate in value. Quiet

residential street. Neighbours friendly or inoffensive. Good friends not too far away. Shopping and services adequate and accessible.

2 Disadvantages

More rooms than we need. Rooms large and expensive to heat. Housework becoming a burden. Reliable domestic help difficult to get and expensive. Garden bigger than we need or can manage. Garden help expensive, if obtainable.

3 Decision to stay or move

Weigh up advantages against disadvantages. Is it a case of sentiment versus saving money and strength? How much is likely to be saved (and/or gained) by selling house and buying or renting another? Take into account legal and removal costs, sacrifices of possessions, replacement of furniture and furnishings, and a float for possible changes in the new home and other contingencies. Consider also the psychological effect of uprooting and the trouble of establishing connections in another environment.

4 If to stay, what changes to make

(a) Divide the house to make a self-contained flat or maisonette for letting. Get advice on feasibility and estimate of cost. Can we afford the outlay? How would the change affect the market value of the house?

(b) Let one or two rooms, furnished or unfurnished, without structural alterations to house. Look carefully into landlord and tenant regulations. If the lodgers proved undesirable, could we get rid of them? Would we find it a burden to provide meals and service? Could we bear to give lodgers the use of the kitchen? Would we hate the invasion of our privacy by strangers?

(c) Share house with members of family or old friends – perhaps another retired couple similarly placed? Can we afford to wait – perhaps years – for the opportunity? Are we likely to be good sharers?

PROS AND CONS OF MOVING

Reasons for moving

To save money and work in a smaller more easily manageable place.
To raise capital on the difference between the sale of the existing home and the purchase (or renting) of another.
To find a more congenial environment.
To be nearer family or friends.

1 *What kind of accommodation*

(a) *Live with relatives*, perhaps with married son or daughter. Requires frank discussion, understanding and tolerance on both sides. If for temperamental or fortuitous reason it ceases to work, the problem of moving will start all over again. We have to be pretty sure of ourselves and the relatives.

(b) *Buy or rent house*. An economic decision: to tie up capital or use the income. Terrace house, semi-detached or detached? — depends on price, whether garage is required, amount of garden space wanted. Bungalow may be more expensive than house with same accommodation, but absence of stairs may be an advantage.

(c) *Housing scheme*. In some areas there are Housing Societies or Associations run by voluntary organizations or co-operatively by the occupiers. The accommodation might be too small or the terms and conditions unacceptable, but I shall ask the local government housing department and CAB for particulars.

(d) *Buy or rent a flat*. More compact than a house and perhaps easier to run, but not necessarily cheaper to buy. Absence of garden may be deciding factor.

(e) *Buy caravan*. Outlay, running costs and rent low by comparison with house or flat. Has advantage of mobility, but will feel rather cramped after living in fairly spacious house. Have always regarded it as holiday accommodation rather than permanent dwelling. However, will look at some catalogues.

2 *Where to live*

(a) *Nearby*. Find smaller place in same locality and so avoid having to change doctor, dentist, bank, etc.

(b) *Further afield*. Go for a complete change. Have several towns in mind, including married daughter's. Must talk this over in detail with wife, then get brochures, and if necessary visit the most promising locations.

(c) *In the country*. We both love the country but have never lived in a village. Will it be too quiet and parochial? What activities would we have to give up? What new interests would we have to acquire? Much would depend upon the size of the village and its proximity to a town with abundant amenities.

(d) *At the seaside*. A fairly large town with mixed occupations would be preferable to a place that subsists only on summer visitors. It would have all the services and amenities of a suitable inland town, plus sea air. The same considerations would apply as in any other location – climate, configuration, transport, cost of living, quality of local government, and one other: is it a congested geriatric refuge?

(e) *Abroad.* Requirements: sunshine, favourable living costs, political stability, no hostility to the British, no insuperable language difficulty, reciprocal health service arrangement with the UK. We should be isolated from family and friends, have to make a new life in an alien society. A trial period out of the holiday season would be instructive, not in a hotel, but self-catering in a rented apartment.

12

Getting Older

Thanks to medical science and the social system, more and more people are living long enough to spend a quarter of their lifetime in retirement. That could be as many years as the span between youth and middle age. There will be changes during those years which our plans should take into account. To be realistic we should divide the period into two parts. One is the still fairly vigorous section from say sixty-five to somewhere in the seventies. The other is the later years when the effects of ageing can no longer be ignored.

We remain in good shape much longer than our counterparts did a generation ago. But longevity has its price. Some years of declining strength and faculties are almost inevitable. With intelligent and unafraid anticipation, life can continue to be worth living. The plan's the thing.

The housing tables in the last chapter referred briefly to the needs of the later years. Stairs might be a trial for rheumatic limbs and necessitate more lifting and carrying than arms and heart could take. Therefore a bungalow or a flat might be better than a two-floor house. The garden should be small and planned to eliminate digging and mowing. You will need a labour-saving house, inside and out.

Eventually, you may need more than that. Is it prudent or morbid to plan in detail for a possible period of decline? Is it just as well to take a chance on future possibilities and disabilities? No one can advise. But there are a few preparations you can make, no matter where or how you live.

Look again at the health chapters. We reminded you that old people are less steady physically and therefore more liable to accidents. It is well known that most accidents occur in the home at all ages. But a fall which sprains an ankle at thirty could break a limb at seventy, when recovery from any accident will be slower. Therefore, as our chapter heading said, look after yourself.

Make changes in the home to reduce risk and strain. If the bath has no hand grips replace it with one which has a grip on each side. Have non-slip flooring in bathroom, toilet and kitchen, and non-slip, non-trip mats and rugs.

Make reaching unnecessary

Rearrange your stores to give access without need to stand on chairs and ladders. Reserve high shelves and cupboards for items seldom if ever used. Better still, redesign storage to make reaching unnecessary. You may be nimble enough in your sixties but you will be glad of the precautions ten years ahead.

Lifting and pushing heavy furniture is not the best kind of exercise for the old. There are gentler ways of keeping fit described in an earlier chapter. If your easy chairs and bed are not on castors have them fitted before the need becomes urgent. Free-standing wardrobes are notorious causes of rupture. Replace them with built-in units. You will eliminate dust traps and save cleaning too.

Central heating is a comfort at any stage in life, but in the later years it can be a life-saver. It has been said that more old people die of hypothermia than the statistics reveal. If increasing fuel costs prohibit heating throughout the house, your rehousing plan should provide a compromise. Be content with smaller accommodation which will cost less to heat. And save heat loss by spending some money on insulation.

Ideally, an old person's home should be evenly heated throughout. Steep changes of temperature are a health hazard. It is usually the bathroom and the toilet — the places where one is most vulnerable to cold — that come off worst in the fuel economy calculations. They should at least have a source of warmth that can be switched on when needed, subject of course to the obvious safeguards for electrical equipment in a damp environment.

Old people who have a nostalgic attachment to coal fires will be obliged sooner or later to weigh up sentiment against labour. Making up the fire on winter mornings and raking out the ashes at night are indulgences for younger and hardier bodies.

Security is important at any age, but the very old are at a special disadvantage. Houses have been entered while the occupants slept or watched television, and impaired hearing increases the risk. There is no complete safeguard. The best one can do is to make breaking-in difficult. The police have security specialists to advise on home safety. There are reliable firms who will locate the danger points and fit protective devices. Look them up in the classified telephone directory.

Unpickable locks on doors, bars on the more vulnerable windows and a chain on the front door are well worth the small cost. Back them up with common sense. Close windows before going out. Don't leave outside doors open in unattended rooms. Don't leave ladders around the house, or other means of access to upper windows.

The greatest danger is the smug feeling that assault and robbery happen to other people. Nowadays no house is too humble to be robbed, no one too poor to be a target. Old age and physical handicap no longer procure immunity.

A telephone must be numbered among the safeguards. It is no mere utility for the very old, but a lifeline for bringing help in emergency. It is also a shield against loneliness. Those who are housebound because of infirmity or weather conditions must have a means of speaking to a friend. Whatever you sacrifice for reasons of economy, don't give up the telephone.

Forethought can make living conditions tolerable up to an advanced age. Some fortunate people can fend for themselves satisfactorily to the end of a long life. Others struggle against disability and still have the hard-bought satisfaction of retaining their home and independence. It is a constant surprise to people who have not yet reached that stage how the will can surmount disabilities.

So long as the will dominates, no one has the right to advise giving in. But it is sensible to accept mechanical aids, of which there are some ingenious examples. They are adaptations of standard tools, to enable people to enjoy gardening without having to bend and to do kitchen work in spite of crippled hands. There are even gadgets for pulling on your shoes without stooping. Your doctor should be able to advise you where to obtain these aids.

NEEDING AND ACCEPTING HELP

There may be a still later stage in growing old when self-help even with gadgets will be inadequate. It is then time to abandon false pride and accept personal aid with a good grace. Growing old involves a succession of compromises with disability. The mental adjustment is painful for many people. In the chapter on morale we spoke of the need for a philosophical acceptance of the facts of ageing. The strain upon philosophy increases as the miseries multiply in the later years. Except in the distress of illness and pain it is possible to make a virtue of necessity, to regard survival as a triumph, not a disaster.

Your attitude to your own condition is reflected in other people's attitude towards you. They will admire instead of pitying. 'Isn't he (she) wonderful! I won't mind growing old if I can be like that,' is the most heartwarming tribute youth can pay to extreme old age.

If you have done voluntary work for one of the charities partly or exclusively concerned with the old and infirm, you will know what will be available to you in a similar predicament. They include the WRVS, the British Red Cross Society, the Council of Social Service, Age Concern, Help the Aged, Leagues of Hospital Friends, and a variety of local welfare organizations formed to supplement the provisions of the National Health Service.

The NHS is concerned strictly with health and the aftermath of sickness. Social security tries more or less successfully to fill the gap in personal finance. But there are personal needs beyond the reach of money and medication. These must be served by unofficial effort. Most of us would rather not be wards of the State, even though the alternative is accepting charity.

The word charity applied to the voluntary organizations is unfortunate but unavoidable. It implies official recognition of a benevolent non-profit-making activity, and exempts the funds from taxation. You should regard it as a technical term without any taint of condescension. You have contributed to the charities in the past. What they do for you in your need may be regarded as society's repayment of some of the debt.

When you worked for a charity you were directly or indirectly a dispenser of benefits. Now you will be a recipient. The difference will be all the more apparent because of the personal contacts involved. By comparison, collecting your pension from the post office and handing your prescription to the chemist are impersonal routines. You will be visited and questioned about your circumstances. You may feel that your secret life is being invaded.

It can be less painful (as well as more blessed) to give than to receive. You will know from experience that voluntary workers are not all angels. Lady Bountiful and Lord High Executive still exist. But the better types predominate. One of the more subtle effects of the Welfare State is that it has taken so much of the curse off voluntary as well as official aid. In time we all become senior citizens. In the fullness of time most of us will need supplementary help. Survival with dignity has become a right.

While some of the voluntary workers are officious and too self-consciously charitable, they have legitimate complaints against some of their clients. The very old can be capricious, exacting and unco-operative. These may be symptoms of senility, calling for patience, cajolery and at times severity on the part of the volunteer. But if they are signs of cussedness there is no excuse. Givers have rights as well as recipients.

In other words, aid should not be a one-way traffic. It is most successful where there is co-operation. However great one's need may be one has to recognize that voluntary organizations are usually overburdened and short of funds and of skilled helpers. They do their best within harassing limitations.

What do they provide? In effect, anything that is not available from the NHS via your doctor, or in cash from the Department of Health and Social Security. You have to seek out the appropriate source of help, and make known your needs.

The nationwide organizations with well-known names, such as the WRVS, are easy enough to find in the directories. They may have branches near your home. But local organizations, with less familiar names, will be more difficult to locate. Your library or the social service department at the town hall may be able to help. Or, as with so many other queries, your most useful source of information will probably be the Citizens' Advice Bureau.

What you will need and where to apply for it will depend on what the years have done to you. The main deprivation will be mobility. You may want occasional private transport when getting in and out of buses becomes a strain. If you are housebound you may need someone to do your shopping. If you are bedridden you will need a meals service and home help.

Obviously, people living alone will be in greatest need. Most of them will be women. They will however be more resourceful than men in coping with the domestic routines. If there was any doubt in early life, there is none in the later years about which is the weaker and the helpless sex.

There is some overlapping of functions among the service organizations. It is not always clear who will provide what. You have to find out ahead of acute need. Another precaution is to arrange with a good neighbour or a friend living nearby to look in from time to time. Try not to worry about 'imposing' upon them or being a burden. They may see your trust as a compliment.

You may decide that you could reduce some of the problems by applying for accommodation under one of the 'sheltered housing' schemes. Sheltered housing bears no relation to the Housing Associations referred to in the last chapter. It is sponsored by various charities (Help the Aged is one of the largest) in many parts of the country. The schemes differ in detail but have the same purpose; to offer independent accommodation in the form of bedsitter or small flat, with varying communal facilities, at a subsidized rental. There is a warden on call for emergencies, and sometimes a resident nurse.

Whatever you do to ease the later years of a long retirement, they must be less comfortable than the early years. They need not be unhappy. If you have faced the shock of retirement successfully, and become reconciled to the inevitability of ageing, you will be well prepared for the disabilities of the later years.

We are reminded of an indomitable lady on her ninety-first birthday. She was in a geriatric ward among other people, many of them younger, who had abdicated from all life's obligations. Partly recovered from a fractured wrist and thigh, she still had the resolution to put on her best clothes, make up her face and sit through a special hair-do for the occasion. 'I've still got my self-respect,' she said.

In the last analysis, the most precious human ingredient seems to be morale. And not only in retirement.

PART THREE

Financing Your Retirement

13

The Question of Finance

So far we have dealt with every feature of retirement except money.
Of course, finance has been implicit in everything that has been said.
We can't enjoy our leisure unless we can afford it, and to that extent
therefore it has to be bought. If income falls short of basic needs we
give up some leisure and seek paid work. In Parts One and Two it has
been assumed that one has contrived to make ends meet and even
overlap a little for comfort and security.

But the problem of how the ends are tied up remains. It has,
advisedly, been left to the last. The management of money and budgeting of expenditure are weighty considerations. They are in some ways
the most complicated elements in retirement planning. They are,
understandably, a considerable source of anxiety for most people
approaching retirement. In Part Three we must look to our financial
resources.

Money is the immediate preoccupation, and remains for some time
the dominant one in thoughts about retirement. By rational standards
health should come first, but the two are closely involved. Money
worries can effect health. We have said enough in other chapters about
the shock of retirement. One's salary comes to an abrupt end. A
pension, perhaps more than one pension, will replace it. But the two
forms of remuneration do not balance. A gap is visible, and it can
widen with the years.

Worrying questions arise. Will I have enough to live on? If it is
enough now, how long will it remain so? How can I provide safeguards against the chances of an obscure future?

The obscurity of the future is one of the trickiest aspects of financial
planning. Some things can be planned early with reasonable accuracy.

E

For instance, how we spend our time is largely in our own hands. But money values are being changed by factors beyond our control. We cannot foresee what inflation will have done to our savings and income in ten, five or even two years from now. Even expert forecasters get it wrong.

Little wonder that to people of moderate means the prospect of retirement may look like perpetual unemployment linked with a losing battle for survival. Their only certainty seems to be that prices will rise. It would help if they knew by how much. We tend to become increasingly resistant to the promises of politicians that national recovery is well on the way.

It is a defeatist attitude, but widespread. It afflicts people at all financial levels, not least those with substantial capital. They have seen their income restricted by dividend restraint, and whittled away by higher rate taxation and the investment income surcharge, while growth is inhibited by capital gains tax, threatened by recurring hints of a capital levy, and what survives eroded by inflation. We have spoken to directors of flourishing businesses in their early sixties who are seriously thinking of retiring to another European country which is kinder to capital and to the income it produces.

Where the comparatively rich panic over retirement, what can the not so rich do? We have said it again and again, but it will bear repeating. Don't leave the problem till retirement day: tearing your hair won't balance your budget. The first essential step is to plan well before the event.

Among the most important reasons for planning early is that you plan from strength. You are ten years younger and that much fitter. You are in a job; you can, we hope, pay your way and have enough peace of mind to think clearly about your future. Time is on your side. We recommended that you submit your personality and life style to a personal audit. Now do the same with your material resources.

It will be less straightforward in this case. In these unsettled times, as we have said, it is difficult to deduce the future from the present. Forecasting is almost a branch of prophesy. But businesses make the attempt and so should we. A glimmer of light must be more revealing than total darkness.

It is tempting to use the uncertainty of the future as an excuse for delaying the plan. One can argue that an attempt to plan finance ten years ahead is unrealistic, and in the end will be a waste of effort. That is a rationalization of unwillingness to be bothered. Let us admit it:

we all have a streak of laziness and are ingenious in justifying pro-crastination. But the business analogy holds true, even though the pressures are less insistent in private life. In neither sphere can one live satisfactorily from day to day.

The chief danger of negligence is that it leaves all the planning to be started at the time when the plans should have matured. Then panic sets in. Decisions are made in a hurry and inadequate or inefficient measures are taken. Retirement is a crisis in our lives only if we fail to face it early and make provision judiciously.

Preparing for the future is not, or should not be, unfamiliar to anyone who is within ten years of retirement. You have been doing it all your life. When you showed a preference for a pensionable job, took out a life assurance policy, embarked on a mortgage, you had a distant future in mind. All saving rests on some plan, however tenuous. As you have grown older, you have learnt how to plan deliberately and more effectively.

STARTING YOUR PLAN

Where do you begin your financial plan? The obvious method seems to be the one you adopted in the personal audit. You will look at the current situation and decide in broad terms how it will differ from circumstances in retirement. In other words: first, where does the money go now; which of these commitments will cease as a result of retirement and which will diminish as a result of ageing; granted health and the means, how would you like to live in retirement? Next, what are your present sources of income, what sources will you have when you retire, what can you do now to secure the necessary resources for the life-style you envisage?

As in the former audit, it helps if you list the items on paper. Put them in parallel columns, so that the changes are apparent at a glance. Leave a column for notes and space for additions and changes as new thoughts occur.

Don't expect the plan to be complete at any stage. It is a guide, not a statutory instrument. Don't hesitate to modify it to fit changes of mind and circumstance. Flexibility is an essential part of the exercise.

Let us look again at the table drafted by our hypothetical planner. But first, let us remember who he is. Or rather who he is not. He has no existence as depicted. He is not a case history or a portrait. He is not and cannot be typical. But he has a kind of reality, as a vehicle for some common characteristics and situations. Each detail of what he is and does applies to large numbers of people. He exists piecemeal, if not as a whole.

His pursuits and interests show him to be middle class. He has the amenities and tastes common to his status – a mortgage nearing completion, a car, an active interest in golf, tennis and swimming. He is in the mid-fifties, becoming aware that he is 'not as young as he was', and cutting down the more exacting activities and indulgences. He is an engineer, no doubt quite a well-paid and pensionable job.

He is a good citizen, an averagely decent family man. His frank self-analysis reveals no vices and no serious defects of character. His life is fairly simple and reasonably happy.

What will he be like as a person in ten years' time? Not fundamentally different. Character and temperament are well established by middle age. It is very unlikely that a man of his type will run wild in retirement. There would have been signs and adventures long before.

In any case, nature provides built-in inhibitors. Failing powers enforce moderation. There are other restraints. The spirit may be willing, but the bank balance weak. On the whole, retirement is a time for sobriety, and sobriety is the supreme money-saver.

What kind of life does our man want when he retires? He tells us a little and we can deduce more. He will still be sociable, but will entertain and be entertained less. He will remain active mentally and physically but concentrate on the less expensive interests. He will do voluntary work, but evidently expects, or at least hopes, that he will not need to work for money.

There is a moral gain from this frank look at himself. He has dropped some of the illusions he may have had about his character, conduct and personality. He is likely to use the same realism in assessing his needs in retirement. What many people might regard as deprivations in the leaner years after sixty-five, will be classed as expendable items in an objective review. Pre-retirement planning is an exercise in philosophy as well as in economics.

Philosophy is not simply passive acceptance of a lowered standard. Standards can change without deteriorating. Life can be austere in retirement and is so for many people. There is no magic in planning, and philosophy cannot work miracles. Nevertheless, an examination of our present circumstances alongside an intelligent estimate of future needs and possibilities can perhaps save us from austerity by default.

That is what we shall try to do in the chapters to come. We shall consider current sources of income and what basic changes retirement will bring. There will be an unavoidable loss of earned income, partly compensated by expected gains in pensions. There will be minor but not negligible gains in the form of age concessions. One of the main variables will be savings and the income from investments. We shall examine ways of improving the financial position by competent management of assets.

Then we shall look at expenditure, and determine which categories will diminish or cease altogether as a direct result of the changed circumstances. Retirement from a full time paid job is the catalyst. Other economies can result from judicious reappraisal of wants and needs. Ageing will be the main determinant.

These calculations will be reviewed periodically to take account of changes. The most troublesome changes will be those which are outside our control and unpredictable. They are imposed by the exigencies of the national economy and the caprice of politicians. They include official restrictions and taxations, and – let us be fair to our masters – an occasional concession aimed specially at the lower paid and the retired.

Finally, we shall try to draw the threads together in a retirement budget; bearing in mind that there are no certainties, but that uncertainty is not completely impenetrable.

14

'What Shall I be Able to Afford?'

The most disturbing question in the mind of anyone thinking about retirement is, 'What shall I be able to afford?' He is probably reconciled to being poorer when earned income ceases, but he wants to know how much poorer. Which of the things he enjoys now will he have to forgo, and will he mind the sacrifice? What kind of life does he want, and how can he achieve it?

Some of these questions are common to people in all grades of affluence. Even the well-to-do are anxious. Some may see their living standard fall to a level that for most of us would be unattainable wealth. But it is still a fall. Impoverishment is relative.

At the other end of the scale poverty is absolute. The really poor are those who have nothing but the state pension and perhaps small savings which will not affect their eligibility for supplementary benefit. Their problem may be less complicated than that of the rich, but it is obviously more acute.

Between those extremes are the not so poor, or the not so rich, according to your point of view. They receive the state pension as a matter of course, and many will have an occupational pension too. They have savings and some investment income. They are entitled to the normal age concessions. But otherwise, like the rich, they must rely on their own resources.

It is from that large and varied middle section that we drew our specimen retirement plan. Our message may seem to apply mainly to that category, but there will be an appreciable overlap on either side.

Superficially, the three classes would appear to have little in common. For instance to the poor, the state pension is the prop upon which their living depends. To the rich, what is left of the pension after tax may not be enough to pay the newspaper bill. To the people in the middle it is not exactly a lifeline, but it is a useful extra, and its absence would be felt.

Despite the differences, all three share a basic priority. Within the boundaries of their needs and ambitions they want financial security and a reasonable standard of living. You may think that is little enough to hope for, or wildly out of reach, according to your circumstances and level of optimism. For most people it will be easy to achieve, and we cannot promise a formula. But we can offer a few guidelines towards a plan. The outcome is partly in your hands, partly at the mercy of chance and politics. By playing your hand with forethought you can do something to circumvent those two formidable barriers.

PRESENT AND FUTURE RESOURCES

What you will be able to afford will depend on three matters within and two outside your control. These are: 1) your present resources 2) how you deploy those resources 3) what you can do to increase them 4) what will be the future value of the provision you make for your retirement, and 5) what additional benefits from external sources will be available when you retire.

Your present resources can be classified broadly under three heads: salary, savings (including investments), and possessions in kind. Your salary will cease on retirement, but your occupational pension may be related to your total earnings or to your earnings in the final years

What is left . . . may not be enough to pay the paper bill

of employment. If you plan early you will have to take into account how your earnings are likely to change before retirement. You may be able to think of ways of improving the final result.

Don't say, 'That's groping in the dark.' All planning takes place in an atmosphere of uncertainty. The purpose of planning is to lighten the darkness a little, or at least to accustom our eyes to seeing into the depths.

Savings are a similar case. You know what they amount to now, but you do not know for how long they will be adequate or whether they will have to be increased to provide for retirement. In most cases it is safe to assume that some increase will be needed. Early planning gives you time and, one hopes, opportunity to make additions.

Possessions in kind cover everything except money. They include house, car, furniture, and that miscellaneous category known as 'valuables'. They are, together with conspicuous expenditure, the outward sign of a living standard. From the point of view of life in retirement there will be redundancies and gaps on the list, but these can be foreseen. We shall tabulate and appraise them as part of the suggested plan.

How will you deploy those resources to ease the stringent conditions of retirement? Your present earned income will affect life in retirement in three ways. The amount of the occupational pension may be linked to it, as we have said. (We shall look at the link in more detail when we come to pensions.) Earned income is a source of saving. It is also a source of further possessions.

Increasing one's income has never been easy, but fresh obstacles have been added to the traditional ones in recent years. Incomes from employment have been subject to an official incomes policy which has inhibited growth irrespective of merit. The self-employed have not been immune. If however you have your own business, your earned income source will also be one of your assets. It is a medium of investment and a means of increasing capital. We shall have a little more to say on the subject under an appropriate heading.

But to return to income. How much you can save out of income depends, of course, upon how much you can spare, but there is a dilemma. You can skimp the present for the sake of the future, or you can live up to the limit and trust to luck for the future. We discounted luck when we agreed on the need for planning. No doubt you will decide, rightly, to compromise. Misers and spendthrifts are born, not made.

On the other hand you may find that, even with the keenest planning, your current needs leave no surplus. The plan should make the position clear. One of the advantages of pre-retirement planning is that it helps us to live sensibly before retirement. Indeed, there is much to be said for planning as part of our way of life. Perhaps we can't start too early.

Possessions in kind are a part of capital. They may represent the bulk of what one owns. An owner-occupier's house, no longer bound by a mortgage, may exceed in value all his other possessions. Whether it is to be retained or sold to release capital is a major decision, to be discussed apart from the disposal of lesser possessions such as furniture. That also applies to the car. Will running costs be more than you can afford? Should you continue to drive? In the case both of house and car, finance may not be the main consideration. Health and the expected disabilities of ageing may prove decisive in the choice of a domicile and a mode of transport.

Minor possessions, what we might call the utilities, will be deployed in accordance with need and circumstance. Obviously a smaller house will accommodate less furniture. If you tend to be a hoarder, you can expect to become more so as you get older. Deciding what to do with furniture and effects can be a worth-while discipline. You can also discipline in advance the old 'accumulator' you may become.

Don't, however, be reckless in your campaign against clutter. You can throw out too much. Some articles can be standbys for other reasons than utility or sentiment. They may have a market value which will appreciate in time. After retirement you might be glad of a few unwanted objects which could be sold for wanted cash.

So, you will try and work out what to save for retirement, what to eliminate, what more you will need. If you can buy some of the necessary additions in advance, you can avoid the almost inevitable rise in prices. It is a safe assumption that no prices will come down.

How can you increase your resources? This is the most difficult of the five questions we have set. For a younger person in a more buoyant economy the answer would be to earn more money, save more money and invest wisely. But those are glib answers today. With earnings that never seem to overtake prices, and savings which, if possible at all, dwindle in value, neither prudence nor wisdom helps us much. Nevertheless, we must do something to mitigate the effects of an adverse economic environment. We shall try to offer advice and comfort, but no false hopes.

The fourth question follows naturally from the third. What will be the value of the provision you make for your retirement? This is where inflation rears its depressing head. The simple answer is that nobody can know. Economists are as much in the dark as we are, and politicians throw dust in our eyes and their own for obvious reasons.

The only facts are in the past. You know how your costs have risen over, say, the last five years. If you have kept records (counterfoils or cheque stubs) you will be able to compare expenditure on the general rate, fuel, telephone and other regular charges. Add whatever other increases you can remember – travel, clothing, holidays, entertainment, food, and the miscellaneous items in the housekeeping budget. Wives, who are the immediate sufferers at the point of sale, have the better memory.

The figures will provide a clue of a kind to future trends. It will be little more than a reasonable guess. Unforeseeable events may halt or accelerate inflation and, for better or worse, make nonsense of our calculations. For safety, one should lean slightly to the side of pessimism. Whatever provision is made for retirement will have to be adjusted in accordance with this estimate of increasing costs.

In retirement you will have whatever you will be able to retain from your present resources, plus accretions acquired in the planning period, minus the income from employment. Pensions will be additional, replacing part of the lost income. There will also be special age concessions, in effect a social bonus for senior citizens. These are at present of two kinds, tax benefits and perquisites.

The Chancellor of the Exchequer, through his budget, tries to temper income tax to the shorn pensioner. The age concession is an increased personal allowance for people born before a given date whose total income does not exceed a stated amount. It is reduced by stages above that amount until it is no larger than the ordinary personal allowance. Among the perquisites are passes available without means tests to pensioners, entitling them to free travel on buses outside peak hours. In London the bus pass also procures a concessionary fare on the Underground. British Rail grant travel at half-fares to holders of a pensioner's pass for which a moderate charge is made.

A concession from private enterprise is women's hairdressing, available at a reduced price at some establishments at certain times on certain days. There is a commercial rather than a philanthropic reason for the concession: it keeps the staff busy at slack periods. Similar concessions are available at many cinemas and dry cleaners.

Some benefits are not exclusively for the old, but for the poor of all ages, and therefore subject to a means test. They include rates rebates from the local council, and supplementary pensions from the Department of Health and Social Security. Supplementary benefits vary according to need, and cover a variety of expenses including help with rent. One does not have to be destitute or living in squalor to qualify.

Apart from the means-tested benefits which make life possible for the recipients, the value of age concessions varies with the individual. To active people who travel a good deal they yield a worth-while indirect addition to income. By the time you retire there may be more official concessions to the aged. Provision for the old is a growing problem with the increase in their numbers and financial difficulties. Whatever your financial position will be, don't hesitate to take advantage of any public handouts. You should regard them as a dividend from society in recognition of a lifetime's work and contribution to the Exchequer.

We have come a little way towards suggesting an answer to your question at the head of this chapter: 'What shall I be able to afford?' We have looked at some problems and glimpsed a few mitigating features. The next stage is to consider your present financial position in relation to your retirement and the kind of life you hope to enjoy.

If you are in the habit of drawing up a personal balance sheet and updating it annually you will have a clear picture of your assets and liabilities, and simple arithmetic will give you a net worth figure. Very few people are, or need to be, as methodical as that. But when you start planning for retirement you want to know where the deficiencies are and where to correct them. For each year up to retirement you have to watch over your capital, income and expenditure as if you were the finance director of a public company and shareholders were looking over your shoulder. There is in fact a shareholder in waiting: your retired self for whose fortune you are responsible.

Let us look now at your gross assets, starting with cash. This will include cash in hand and in current and deposit accounts at your bank. When retirement is imminent there may be a much bigger cash item. If you decide to commute part of your occupational pension you will have a substantial sum to dispose of. The decision whether to take the lump sum or the pension – and if the lump sum, what to do with it – may have to be left till the pension matures, but you will give some thought to the subject as part of your pre-retirement planning. We shall say more about this when we consider pensions in the next chapter.

If you have an endowment insurance policy, the decision about disposal of the proceeds will similarly have to await maturity. Your list of assets will include Premium Bonds, money invested in the National Savings Bank, National Savings Certificates, building societies, unit trusts, local authority loans, gilts and equities, and a business or professional practice if any.

As far as possible you should estimate the cash value of your assets, including that of property, car and other vehicles, goods and chattels. This will give you a figure of gross worth, from which you will deduct taxation and other liabilities (mortgage payments, hire purchase, overdrafts, etc.) to arrive at a net figure.

These figures will help you to review your capital policy. Have you invested to best advantage? Should you have aimed more at income than growth, or vice versa, in the light of approaching retirement? Have you too many long-term commitments? If you still have a mortgage, should you redeem it now or let it run to the end? We shall raise these questions again in another chapter and try to find the answers.

Changes you make in the disposition of your assets may affect your income and expenditure pattern. Let us look at the current position and allow for those possibilities.

Your income may come from more than one source. Employment (or self-employment) normally accounts for the largest part. If you are an employee (the term covers most directors as well as their subordinates) you may have reached the limit of possible advancement in the job. You may also be too old to risk or even to procure a move to richer pastures. If official income limitations still prevail and living costs continue to rise, you may find that your earned income is static or actually shrinking in purchasing power. You are familiar with the predicament. Those who are not are favourites of the gods and government, or basking under more generous fiscal systems.

You may have other sources of earned income, such as rents and earnings from side-lines. There will probably be small tax-free sums from deposits in the National Savings Bank and from Save as You Earn. Unearned income will be liable to investment income surcharge in addition to income tax at the basic or the higher rate, according to the size of your total income. You can in fact list your gross income from all sources by keeping a duplicate of the particulars you have given in your income tax return.

Let us assume you have deducted from your net income after tax all the payments which are fixed in amount and usually covered by standing order at your bank. They will include mortgage, hire purchase and other forms of credit. You will also deduct bank loan and overdraft repayments. What is left will be the money you will live on: the personal and household 'purse'.

A list of these living expenses will not only show you how you live now, but will help you to estimate how you will live in retirement. You will see which areas of expenditure will disappear when you retire; which you can eliminate or reduce without being seriously deprived; and what items will have to be added to suit the new circumstances. You will then have some idea (subject to the vagaries of inflation) of what you will be able to afford.

WHERE THE MONEY GOES

Now for the pre-retirement list, starting with the house. (Since we are talking of expenditure out of income we shall omit new capital outlay.) If the house is rented, rent may well be your largest single item of expenditure. If you have completed a mortgage you have the comfortable feeling that no one can take the roof from over your head. You still have a rates bill, perhaps rising alarmingly. Even the water rate, too small to notice a few years ago, now makes an appreciable addition. For most people a lump sum advance payment of the general rate is no longer possible, or advisable. You can arrange instalment payments without extra charge.

Heating and lighting are formidable costs. Central heating has been upgraded from a luxury to a necessity. Like most of us you must have sought advice from time to time on comparative costs of fuels and systems in the hope of changing for the better, and ended up – bewildered – where you started.

House maintenance has the double function of preserving the structure and keeping up appearances. You can cut down on the aesthetics, but you will be wise not to risk structural deterioration. A handyman (or woman) can save the cost of labour, but it is worth-while to put some of the savings into better quality materials. Decoration is not an annual event, but it should be budgeted annually, and allowance made for increasing costs over the three- or four-year decoration cycle.

Fortuitous maintenance costs, covering repairs and renovations, are best omitted from these calculations. There should be a reserve to take care of contingencies such as loose covers or curtains that have perished, and any major failure in kitchen equipment no longer under guarantee.

Domestic equipment

This is mainly the phalanx of electrical aids without which no kitchen is considered fully furnished. Running costs are generally low but servicing is becoming more and more expensive. The economics of some of these machines is debatable, but the convenience seems to be beyond doubt. We are reluctant to reduce the number even when the devil drives, but add new ones with pleasure if we can possibly raise the money.

The only electrical device that doesn't reside in the kitchen is the television. If you have not bought it, you pay an annual rental charge, either in instalments or in a lump sum at a reduction. In a class apart among the household devices is the telephone. Like gas and electricity it brings you a quarterly bill.

Insurances

Your house and its contents are of course insured. Premiums increase (or should do so) as the cost of rebuilding and refurnishing rises. Insurance companies tell us by how much when they send us the annual renewal notice, and it is not just sales talk. Under-insurance is false economy, as anyone whose house has been ransacked or destroyed knows. No doubt you have car insurance and perhaps also a life or endowment policy. All told, the premiums add substantially to your outgoings.

A long chapter could be filled with the problems of insurance alone; but one of these is particularly difficult: how to value the contents of your house for insurance purposes. For instance, what would be the replacement value of the dining suite you bought twenty or thirty years ago? You might search the furniture shops in vain for a comparable one so that you can base your estimate on the current price. You could of course call in a valuer – several valuers in fact, since they tend to specialize. But professional valuation is expensive, and usually feasible only if you have what you believe to be some truly valuable possessions. Most of us have to rely on reasonable guess-work supported with whatever we can glean from current prices of the nearest equivalent goods.

It is not only for insurance purposes that you need to value your possessions. When you retire you will want to know what you are worth in cash and goods. If you take the trouble to make an estimate when you start your plan, you can update it annually in the light of specific changes in value or the general inflation figure.

Next on our list of current outgoings are business expenses. Not the current expenses of a business, but the incidental day-to-day costs of going to work. These include travel to the work-place (the season ticket can be a major expense); meals out (there is usually a charge even for canteen food); participation in the firm's activities; club and possibly trade union contributions. The place of work is a community and imposes social obligations.

Domestic help – a nearly extinct species

Housekeeping

Like most of us you provide for the weekly purchases of food, materials and incidentals with a regular allowance. It ranks with the mortgage payments as one of the big expenses. It tells you what inflation is doing to you more accurately and more quickly than the official figures. Trying to hold it down is one of life's losing battles. If you employ domestic help – a nearly extinct species – you can add another front to the battle. Otherwise, cleaning must devolve upon one or both of the domestic partners.

Food absorbs the largest part of the housekeeping allowance even in the smallest households. In order to have a realistic account of food costs you should include non-business meals out and of course extra food and drink for entertaining in the household food bill.

Meals and entertaining on the job should be listed separately, since they cease with the job and have no bearing on retirement.

The car

For most people a car is, next to the house, their most costly single possession. Running costs can be almost as much as those for the house. In fact a car is expensive if it merely stays in the garage. Licence, insurance and depreciation are incurred whether you use the car frequently, little or not at all. The car repays something if you drive to work. But if your work-place is in a congested city centre you may find it worth-while to travel by public transport, and reserve the car for long-distance business calls and leisure motoring.

Transport costs should be viewed as a whole, in order to determine accurately the economics of running and maintaining the car. You will then be able to decide whether the car justifies its keep, or should be replaced with a more economical one, or sold and a car hired when needed. If the car is sheer luxury and you can afford it, count your blessings instead of the cost.

Clothing

This is one of the great variables in family budgets. Some people, and not only the female of the species, are very clothes-conscious. Others, usually the male of the species, are – judging by their appearance – completely clothes-unconscious. Most of us come between the two, with a leaning towards conventional standards. As a retirement planner 'getting on in years' you will have ceased to be either a glass of fashion or ostentatiously shabby (if you were ever either).

What a man spends on clothes depends partly on taste but also on social compulsion – the kind of work you do, the kind of street you live in, the habits and prejudices of your friends. The cost is increased if you are hard on clothes or neglect to look after them. Dry cleaning should be taken into account, as should hire of dress clothes.

Most of these criteria apply also to women, but fashion adds a dimension. A man can be more ruthless in clothes economy than his wife can, though in her case the economics of dress are more subtly calculated and decided.

Clothes are not the only accessories to a presentable appearance. The cost of grooming, especially for women, is substantial enough to be worth listing separately. Most men of retirement-planning age are satisfied with the periodical trim and shampoo, though even here the cost is not negligible. If nature has left enough hair and vanity, we can add a percentage for styling. Hairdressing and cosmetics are typical of a large number of minor purchases which are deceptively trivial when viewed item by item. You could be surprised at what they amount to in a year.

Entertainment

Here the expense is incurred in two directions – self (including wife) and others. Few people know how much their expenditure on theatres, cinemas, concerts, exhibitions, and sports events amounts to in a year. Housewives are aware of the additional strain on the household allowance of entertaining in the home. You may not wish to reduce these pleasures and social obligations, but it is useful to know where the money is going now in order to plan as painlessly as possible for a retired future.

Christmas expenses are big enough to merit special listing. They have to be planned and provided for, like weddings and special anniversaries. They differ, of course, in being an annual event. And, as with everything else, inflation swells the cost.

Among the social as well as family obligations are birthday and wedding presents. The cost of gifts is a harsh revelation of rising costs in general. Do you remember what a shock it was to realize that a fiver no longer bought a present that either did justice to the young couple or kept you level with the more affluent or generous Joneses? Weddings are rare enough for expenditure on the gift to be put into a miscellaneous or 'non-recurring' column. Birthdays are another matter. They not only recur but in many families also multiply. We all know the agony of deciding at what age nieces and nephews can be crossed off the list with impunity.

Sport and hobbies

As one gets older, physical activity diminishes in vigour but not necessarily in cost. For instance, you may retire from the harriers and take up golf. Leisure pursuits involve club and society subscriptions and expenditure on gear, equipment and materials. Some of the outlay is casual and goes unrecorded. You note the cost of a new camera, but probably still take films and processing in your stride. Garden tools, plants and professional pruning are expensive, and gardeners are beginning to find that the cost of seeds is no longer negligible.

Gambling is a hobby or a vice according to one's moral attitude or the degree of addiction. It is an expense by any standards. Even moderate patronage of the betting shop or the bingo hall can result in a sizable overall deficit after subtracting winnings from the total annual stake. You may not want to abstain or even to reduce the indulgence, but it is worth-while to keep an account, if only as a guide to profit and loss.

Personal expenses

The French have a more accurate and vivid expression for pocket money purchases. They call them *les menus plaisirs*. These small pleasures are mostly too trivial to record, and most people would find the exercise a bore. But if you are a smoker the cost of the pleasure will not be small. The annual total can be a shock even for a moderate smoker. Perhaps it is a mistake to lose sight of the smokes bill among the oddments of expenditure, such as postage stamps and parking fees. It is usually big enough to stand alone, like the telephone or the electricity account.

Whether drink should be similarly separated depends on the size of the thirst. For some drinkers it can be, in money terms, one of the *grands plaisirs*.

Holidays

How many holidays do you have a year? If it is one big event, you are already in the habit of weighing up the cost well in advance and making provision. But if you take occasional long weekends in addition, don't omit to include them in the total figure. Otherwise you will not be able to plan economies realistically. Getting last year's value without this year's inflationary addition to cost is still possible if you shop around in the competitive market. Beating the price trend adds zest to the holiday.

You needn't travel with the crowd. You may have a bigger choice at lower cost by taking holidays out of season. Cheap winter holidays are worth considering.

Newspapers and books

You probably pay your newspaper bill weekly or monthly and throw away the chits. Keep them in future and total them at the end of the year. Prices rise by what seem such small amounts that they make no immediate impact. You don't worry about an extra penny or two. But the annual total shows you how insidiously pence mount up to pounds. At today's newspaper and magazine prices it is wise to go over the list and see if there are any you still buy out of habit but no longer read.

Books are a different matter. They are not ephemera, not expendable. Do you buy books you want to read, or books you have read and want to own? The latter is the more economical, but it is helped by access to a well-stocked public library. In any case, at today's prices books are no longer a casual purchase. Do you remember when you could afford to buy a paperback for the journey and leave it in the train?

Charities

Unless you have covenants or subscribe to charities by cheque you probably have no record or remembrance of your benefactions. We would not advise making a note of the modest sums you hand out at the door. You can, however, make an annual estimate to add to the main list. You can keep it for the record, even if you don't intend to use it as a basis for cuts.

Health

The National Health Service does not cover all the costs of health maintenance and sickness, even for retirement pensioners. If you have not retired you will have to pay part of the costs of new glasses, dental treatment and the supply of false teeth, and also pay prescription charges. The charges vary with changes in the national budget. Many people choose to pay for health care by subscribing to BUPA or other sickness insurance schemes. The size of your medical bill depends therefore on your state of health, freedom from accident and from addictive consumption of pills. Even when the cost of surgery, treatments and medicines is largely covered by the NHS, you may need special diets and care which can be expensive. Health is incalculable. You can't budget for chance. The best you can do is to estimate on the generous side and hope to be proved a pessimist.

You have listed your assets, sources of income and expenditure, and you are updating the account annually. How can this exercise help you to estimate what you will be able to afford in retirement?

First, it will show the changes in sources of income when regular paid employment has ended. Second, it will force you to look at your capital from a new angle: how to build and invest it in order to reduce the income gap on retirement. Third, it will make you aware of changed needs in retirement, and consequent changes in the amount and the pattern of expenditure.

Let us start with expenditure. We have itemized your current, pre-retirement, outgoings. Now let us consider them from the point of view of a retired person, say, our hypothetical planner. And let us tabulate the details in much the same way as we did other aspects of his plan.

WHAT YOU SHOULD BE ABLE TO AFFORD

Dwelling place	Paid-up mortgage	You will be sole owner of the roof over your head. Whether you can afford to tie up such a valuable asset is a major consideration. But it is comforting to know that if income falls short of needs, you can realize on the house. (Disposal of assets, including the house, is discussed in the next chapter.)
	Rates	The rates bill for a house that exceeds your requirement is by that much an extravagance. If you can afford it, well and good. But if you have to cut costs, the house property can provide the means. Not only the rates but heating, lighting, decoration, cleaning and everything covered by the term maintenance will, of course, cost less if you move to a smaller dwelling.
	Heating and lighting	You will need more heat relative to space when you retire. Older people feel the cold more acutely, are less active physically, spend more time at home. Though there is no such thing as cheap heating, you can of course keep costs down by heating less space, but also, if you have central heating, by choosing a flexible system. Lighting, like heating, will cost relatively more in one's later years. Eyes need stronger artificial light as one gets older.
	Maintenance (decoration and and cleaning)	You will have the leisure to do most of the decoration yourself. Given the health and strength and a good amateur level of skill you should be able to save labour costs at least on

interior work. Cleaning involves less skill and more muscle, but that too you should be able to do yourself (perhaps you always have).

Housekeeping	Food and household materials	One eats or should eat less in old age. One has fewer meals out and more at home. But that is as far as we can calculate relative costs between now and retirement. Inflation makes the food bill more difficult to calculate than many others. We can skimp decoration and clothing and opt for a genteel shabbiness, but adequate nutrition must be maintained. The best we can do is revise our estimate year by year up to the eve of retirement.
Furniture and equipment	This includes all the kitchen equipment – cooker, refrigerator, freezer, vacuum cleaner, dishwasher, washing machine, etc.	Part of your provision for retirement will be enough furniture and furnishings to avoid costly renewals or additions. You will also have enough kitchen equipment, perhaps more than you will need. The larger items will be covered by servicing contracts, which are worth-while but expensive. Will you need all the equipment? For instance, if you entertain much less, can you dispense with the dishwasher? You may decide you may no longer afford the total luxury of mechanization.
Telephone		For reasons which we have explained elsewhere, this is one item of equipment which you must contrive to afford. It may not cost less than for the non-retired. You may not make more calls, but they may be longer as the telephone becomes a major means of keeping contact. You can save something by telephoning at off-peak periods. You may even succeed, where thousands have failed, in timing and limiting your calls.

The car		Since the car is one of the big sources of expense, it provides one of the chief means of saving. You can use it less and economize on fuel, or get rid of it and save the whole burden. The car is one of the expendable accessories of life, and one of the most easily measurable in money terms. You are in no doubt about what it costs you and what you can save.
Insurances	House and contents, life policy, car insurance, accident insurance	You will have to keep up house and contents insurances after retirement. If you move to a smaller dwelling, get rid of some of the contents, and give up the car, your expenditure on insurance will be reduced accordingly. You may have a life policy with limited premiums, or an endowment policy maturing before you retire. Look at your policies to see if you are covered for accident. There will be an age limit at entry and you may be too old by retirement day.
Entertaining and entertainments	Parties and hospitality; attendance at theatres, cinemas, concerts and spectator sports; television	Hospitality can be adjusted to your means at any time of life, and the retirement period is no exception. Most of your guests will be in similar circumstances and will understand. Retirement is a face-saving excuse for cutting expenditure. As for outside entertainments, you will not buy more than you can afford. For many events, television and radio will provide an acceptable, even a welcome, substitute for attendance. Instead of chafing at increasing licence and hire charges, you should regard them as an economy.
Holidays and transport		Whether or not you continue to run a car, you can make use of age concessions on public transport. Your

time is your own, so you can avoid the crowds and the high season costs on holiday.

Clothes and grooming		By the time he retires a man usually has enough outer wear to supply his needs for years. He can relax the formality in the absence of business obligations. A business woman cannot abdicate to the same extent in retirement, but her clothes will last better when freed from the wear and tear of daily transport and the work-place. Good grooming, as we have pointed out, is important for morale, but, as women with good taste know, a great deal can be achieved with modest expenditure on toiletries and treatment.
Leisure activities	Sport, hobbies, clubs and societies	You will have more time for leisure activities and may spend more money on them. On the other hand, you may actually make money out of a hobby. The garden may cost less than before retirement according to where and how you decide to live. You will at least have a full stock of tools, including a powered mower to save your strength even on a minimal lawn.
Health	Including care of eyes and teeth	It is advisable to keep up your subscription to BUPA or similar scheme. You will need the cover more in the later years. If you need new glasses, you will decide, in accordance with your means and tastes whether to have the NHS kind or pay the high cost of something more elegant. Dental treatment is not cheap on the NHS, but at market prices the cost can be staggering. Ask your dentist what he can do for you on the NHS. Unlike the family doctor a dentist is allowed to

		combine a private with a National Health practice, and can decide which he can afford to offer.
Miscellaneous (personal)	Comprising cigarettes, tobacco, drinks, and casual purchases of all kinds	Apart from smokes and perhaps drinks, these oddments of expenditure are not easily accounted for. You can, of course, keep the total expense under control. The best way is to give yourself a fixed weekly amount of pocket money and, without being too ridiculously meticulous, try to keep within bounds.

What kind of picture emerges from this estimate? It shows a more restricted life than you have now, but age is restrictive. You can't do as much as you did. You don't need as much as you did. So circumstances contrive a balance, within which you can live happily.

We must beware of smugness. Cutting expenditure *does* mean some lowering of standards, and there will inevitably be regrets. The reduced standard is noticeable, and no one likes to betray impoverishment. There is however an escape route. People expect you to have less money in retirement. They understand the disabilities of pensioners, particularly those whose pension is not index-linked. One can be poorer in retirement without losing face.

The heading to our table differs from that at the beginning of this chapter. It suggests not what you will, but what you should, be able to afford. The difference will be resolved by the amount of your income in retirement, and what you can do in this pre-retirement period to augment it judiciously. That is what we shall discuss in the next chapter.

15
Providing for Retirement

Now that you have calculated what kind and quality of retirement you believe desirable and possible, let us look again at the resources which will contribute to that end. In other words, what income can you expect and where will it come from? What will you live on when you retire?

In the front-line of expenditure is cash: cash in hand and close at hand. It is the fast-flowing element in liquidity. It covers the running costs, and contrives to keep the running smooth.

Most people hold just enough liquid funds for current needs. You don't allow cash to lie idle. You make it work for your living. Therefore you keep no more than a reasonable sum in hand and in the bank. Your current account has the advantage of immediate availability, but pays no dividends. No doubt you also have a deposit account, which constitutes a back-up fund from which to replenish your current account. It is quickly accessible, and earns whatever interest the changes in the market rates allow.

There are other, occasional, cash acquisitions which we shall deal with under appropriate headings. These are lump sums from the commutation of an occupational pension, or from an endowment policy, or from the proceeds of a sale. They rank as capital rather than cash.

Cash, then, in the strict sense of the term, is an incidental and evanescent resource, derived from income. For most retired people the pension is a major (often the main) source of income. You may have more than one pension, but one will be a virtual certainty. That is the National Retirement Pension – the 'old age' pension of less delicate, more matter-of-fact times.

PENSIONS

Let us remind you briefly of the details. Everyone who has paid the required number of national insurance contributions becomes eligible for the flat-rate pension. But since it is a retirement pension you have to be retired before you can get it. If men and women stay in a full-time job after sixty-five and sixty respectively they can't claim the state pension. The reason for this is the existence of what amounts to a means test. It is known as the earnings rule.

According to this rule your pension will be reduced for every pound you earn over a stated amount during the first five years after you attain pensionable age. (The limit is raised from time to time in line with increased living costs.) While, therefore, you are permitted to take your pension and still do some part-time work, you may have to be satisfied with a reduced pension. In fact you may find that you are earning enough to wipe out the pension altogether.

The rule applies to men aged sixty-five to seventy and women aged sixty to sixty-five. Only when you have turned seventy (sixty-five in the case of a woman) does the pension become yours without deductions. You are then entitled to the whole sum, no matter how much money you earn or how much you possess.

Because of the earnings rule many senior citizens who want to remain in paid occupation after the official pensionable age prefer not to accept the pension till they reach seventy and sixty-five respectively. They are compensated with a small increase in the rate of pension – as it were a bonus for patience. When therefore the Department of Health and Social Security notifies you, a few months before you reach pensionable age, that the day of decision is approaching, you will be able to tell them that you prefer to await the age when all earnings penalties cease.

Before making a decision you will have to be confident that you can earn enough to justify deferring your pension. You will lose five years' pension payments (less any earnings rule deductions) at the normal rate, and will set against it the addition to the pension that you will receive in subsequent years. If you prefer to work anyway, the gamble is no doubt worth paying for.

There are normally two rates of pension, for single persons and for married couples. The married rate is not double the single rate. A wife who has not qualified for the full rate by her own national insurance contributions is eligible for the pension in respect of her husband's contributions, but her portion of the joint pension is smaller than the full single rate. Only if she has been employed and has enough contributions to her credit does she get the full pension in her own right.

You may find you are entitled to a little extra as a result of a graduated pension scheme for employed persons which started in 1961 and was abandoned in 1975. It may give you a pound or two a week over and above your flat-rate pension. The DHSS should inform you of the graduated pension fragment due with their reminder of your approaching retirement. If they omit to do so, ask for particulars. You may as well have it, if it only buys a couple of beers a week.

The state pension is not automatically linked to the cost of living index, but the government increases it from time to time under political pressure and economic compulsion. This provides some protection against inflation. The pension is not, and is not intended to be, enough to live on by itself. In spite of budgetary boosts it tends to slip behind the rise in prices. Those for whom it is virtually the sole income can apply for supplementary benefit. This helps with such burdens as rent and extra heating in winter, and aims to bring the income up to subsistence level.

Most people draw their pensions weekly on demand, or at longer intervals within prescribed limits, by presenting their pension book at a post office. If you can afford to wait you can arrange to be paid quarterly in arrears by post.

In most cases the pensioner's position under the national scheme is clear. But sometimes advice may be required, as for instance when a wife reaches pensionable age before her husband, or if you retire early and want to know whether you are eligible for unemployment pay. When in doubt you can call at your local DHSS office and get the answers from the available literature or personally from officials.

You cannot predict what your state pension will be worth by the time you retire. Pensions legislation changes, and can affect company pensions as well as the state provisions. As part of your pre-retirement planning you should watch the newspapers for information and interpretations.

Change has speeded up in recent years. When life and politics were simpler we had an annual budget in April. Now we have additional 'mini-budgets' and special packages of legislation in between. You might find it useful to start a newspaper clipping file as a hedge against confusion.

Occupational pensions, long established in the public service, are spreading throughout the private sector. The number of people entitled to two pensions is now well into eight figures. There are many kinds of scheme, all differing from the state pension and, in commerce and industry especially, varying widely among themselves.

The sixty-five/sixty age rule, universal and inflexible for the state pension, does not apply everywhere for occupational pensions. It is accepted for the most part in industry and commerce for reasons of expediency, but retirement age is sixty for both sexes in the Civil Service and less in the police force. Some industries, both public and private, follow government and local government practice. In both sectors there has been powerful lobbying, with in some cases warnings of more forceful measures, to procure a lowering of the retirement age. Pension policy is in a ferment.

Early retirement presents special problems. In the interval up to state pension age you may be officially regarded as unemployed, and eligible, for part of the period at least, to unemployment benefit. You may also have to keep up your National Insurance contributions. By registering for a job at your local Job Centre you will be credited with the contributions needed to complete your entitlement eventually to the state pension. The position is usually obscure and full of pitfalls. You should get it cleared up at the local office of the Department of Health and Social Security.

There are fewer early retirement (and other) pension problems for Civil Servants. For instance, Civil Service pensions are protected against inflation automatically, and therefore more precisely than the state pension. There is as yet no such statutory protection for occupational pensions in the private sector.

State pensions are paid without tax deduction. They are not, of course, tax free, though this is not always realized. All pensions count as earned income and are subject to income tax like any other earnings.

If you are employed in an organization which has a pension scheme, are you sure that you know exactly what your entitlement will be? If you are a public servant, the issue will probably be clear-cut. It may not be so clear if it is one of the varied and often involved systems in private enterprise. As part of your planning, read the details again in the staff handbook or pension book. And if there are still obscurities don't neglect to ask the executive in charge of pensions for clarification.

So far there has been no national standard for occupational pensions. Integration of state and occupational pensions is brought nearer by the government's new two-part pension scheme applicable to people who are in employment after 6 April 1978. One part corresponds to and replaces the flat-rate retirement pension, the other is an additional earnings-related pension, and both are protected against shrinkage of buying power through inflation. Companies have been given the option of staying in the scheme or, subject to certain conditions, contracting out. The advantages and disadvantages of both courses, and the complications either way, have been debated in board rooms, staff associations and trade unions, and decisions agreed, for better or worse, by management and rank and file.

Almost all occupational pension schemes have been based in some way on earnings. Most of them are calculated on final pay together with the number of years you have been in the scheme. Final pay is usually taken to be the average of the last three years. The pension will then be, say, one-sixtieth (or in some cases one-eightieth) of final pay for each year in the scheme. The higher the final pay, of course, the higher the pension. Some pensions may amount to two-thirds of the last three years' average.

Other schemes use variations of the method, such as the average of the last five years, or of the best three consecutive years, or an average based on the number of years' service at each level of pay. Some of the calculations are very involved. No doubt there is someone in the accounts department able to help you with them.

Some companies make a deduction for the state pension, but this does not necessarily mean that you get a smaller final pension. It does suggest, however, that you should enquire how you stand. Enquire also whether the pay on which your pension is calculated includes extras such as commission, bonuses and overtime. Some companies include them, some stick to basic pay.

Most pension schemes are contributory, the employer paying the larger portion. In most cases employees cannot choose whether or not to join the scheme. Acceptance of employment involves acceptance of the pension provisions.

Usually the scheme provides cover for sickness and disablement, and makes provision for widows. Do you know what your wife would get in the event of your death in harness, or after retirement? Does the scheme permit you to make extra provision for her by sacrificing part of your own pension? If you decided to retire before the age laid down in the company's rules, how much would you lose? Could you draw a proportion of the full pension, or would you have to accept a deferred pension? Will your pension increase after retirement to take account of inflation (some private sector pensions do) and, if so, to what extent? The details are in the booklet supplied to every employee. It makes essential rather than enthralling reading. You have only yourself to blame if you remain in ignorance.

If you have changed jobs you will have lost some pension benefit. More than one change will have set you back considerably. The universally transferable pension has yet to come. There are several forms of carry-over. The old and the new employer may have been able to arrange a transfer because their schemes were compatible. Or you may have had a refund of your contributions in a lump sum. Or you may have a preserved pension from your former employment, which means that you cannot claim it till you reach retirement age. It will not have been preserved against inflation, and may not be worth much when you get it.

Many employed people can expect no occupational pension. They either work for very small employers or are self-employed. The self-employed (professional people, plumbers, one-man shopkeepers, freelance journalists, directors of family businesses) must make their own pension arrangements. If you are self-employed you may have taken steps to supplement the state pension by an annuity, endowment policy or other kind of personal pension plan offered by insurance companies. The government encourages them with tax concessions. Some of these schemes are complex and not easy to evaluate without expert guidance. Your bank manager should be able to help you sort out the complexities.

How to augment your pensions should be a major consideration in pre-retirement financial planning. There is a sense in which all unearned income in retirement is an addition to pension. It has the disadvantages of fluctuating with the vagaries of the market, and incurring a tax penalty at the higher income level in the form of the investment income surcharge.

As retirement approaches, you may have the problem of deciding how best to use one or more substantial sums of money due to you or available at your discretion. Some occupational pension schemes bring you a lump sum in addition to the pension. In other cases you have the option to commute part of the pension for a lump sum. Find out what the company's rules are about commutation. In any case, the process is irreversible. You have to decide whether the present gain is worth the sacrifice of a pension in the future.

Don't commute unless you have a plan for using the money to better advantage than taking the full pension. If the pension is index-linked you might be unwise to disturb it. If it is not, its value will fall as money values have done for decades. You could live to see it shrink from a substantial part of your total income to mere pocket money. Is it wise, then, to opt for a lump sum?

That depends on what you intend to do with it. We shall assume that you won't want to start a business at sixty-five – though that would not be unprecedented. It would of course nullify your retirement. There might be worse consequences. Success could be as embarrassing as failure. The business could get out of hand, exhaust your strength. Perhaps you have a profitable leisure interest of a kind already described which you could finance with the money. But you would still be giving large parts of your pension as a hostage to fortune.

If on the other hand you can afford to spend the money on a bigger car or a boat, well and good; but don't forget the possibly inflation-haunted old fellow whose income you are milking to provide present luxuries. You can invest the money for income or growth, according to your present and estimated future needs. (We shall have something to say shortly about investment.) Or you may decide to put it towards the purchase of an annuity.

The two main facts about an annuity are that you have to surrender the capital sum, and that you receive the annuity for the rest of your life. If you live long enough you can get your capital back – and more. You have, in fact, bought a pension outright. The sum you receive annually (or by arrangement half-yearly) is made up partly of a return of capital and partly of income. The capital portion is tax free; the income portion has income tax deducted at source at the standard rate. Apart from variations attributable to changes in income tax, the sum does not change. Since, therefore, it is not index-linked, its value is vulnerable to inflation.

Because you have handed over the capital sum, you are likely to get a more generous return than from an investment at the prevailing interest rates. This might outweigh the fact that the capital sum if invested would have continued to have a value, however attenuated by inflation and the hazards of the share market. Insurance companies differ in the annuity terms offered and it is worth-while to shop around and take every little advantage. Your bank manager can help you here.

Annuities are for the elderly. The yield increases with age at entry. You will get much better terms by buying an annuity at seventy than you would have done at sixty. Annuities are also for people without dependents. If you have no one to leave the money to, you won't regret giving it to the insurance company. The situation is different for a married couple. A spouse might decide that a lump sum dwindling in value would be less useful to the survivor than an addition to pension. In that case an arrangement can be made for a reduced annuity to be paid during the annuitant's lifetime in return for continuing payments at the same rate for the lifetime of the surviving partner.

Deciding whether the advantage, balanced against the disadvantages, of an annuity justify commuting part of your pension is not, as you will have gathered, simply a matter of arithmetic. We live in indeterminate times and face an unpredictable future. In these circumstances it is wise to accept the outcome of your own judgement and not spend energy afterwards in futile doubts and regrets.

You may have other lump sums coming to you in the planning years: a maturing endowment, or a legacy, or, miraculously, a winning Premium Bond. If you don't want to buy or increase an annuity you will have to decide what else to do with the money.

HOUSE PROPERTY

One action you may want to consider is the redemption of your mortgage. We have assumed that the mortgage still has a few years to run, and that it will be completed in any case by the time you retire. Is anything to be gained by hastening the process?

At that late stage it is sensible to let the mortgage take its course. The interest element is very much smaller than in the early years, and each instalment represents a sizable repayment of borrowed capital out of income. One reason for wanting to shed the mortgage may be impatience. You may feel that your finances will look tidier without it. If dipping deeply into capital for emotional reasons seems to you worth-while, go ahead. But at least be clear about your motives.

The case is different if you are some distance – ten years or more – from the termination of your mortgage, and can see it continuing into your retirement. You may then want to unload the burden before you retire. The economics of repaying a mortgage is determined by the prevailing interest rates. If you would have to borrow at a higher rate than the mortgage interest in order to repay the mortgage you might decide to leave well alone. The same would apply if you had to draw on capital earning higher interest than you were paying on the mortgage. Much would depend on changes in interest rates generally, in building society rates, and in income tax concessions for mortgagees.

It is impossible to generalize on these matters. Cases differ in too many ways. The one constant is the importance of examining the proposition all round as part of the pre-retirement plan. Implicit in the decision will be the need to maintain liquidity. You will want to repay as many debts as possible before retirement. A mortgage is after all one of the biggest of the debts.

A more positive way of providing for retirement is to sell an unwanted asset. If you own another house you may want to hold it for a time as a possible alternative dwelling for retirement. If it is a cottage in the country you may think of moving there eventually and selling the town house. If it is a seaside chalet it could save you hotel bills on holiday and yield income from lettings at other times. The decision to sell might have to be deferred.

The state of the property market could force the issue. You could cash in on a boom. The snag is that one doesn't always recognize a boom till the slump comes, and there's no profit in hindsight. You may of course need the money in any case, and if the market looks favourable you will have to suppress agonizing speculation as to whether it might go higher.

Don't forget that the sale of the second house will attract Capital Gains Tax. If the house you live in is your sole property and you sell it to move elsewhere, the transaction is exempt from CGT. But in the eyes of the law the other house represents wealth, and cashing in carries a penalty. We shall return to the subject of CGT when talking about investment.

There is another penal tax which may descend on your head. This is Capital Transfer Tax. If in clearing the decks for a retired life you wanted to give away some assets, your benevolence could be costly. There are exceptions: for instance gifts and legacies however large between husband and wife escape CTT outright. But a business interest which you wanted to hand over to your son, an antique or work of art (unless, within certain limits, intended as a wedding present) for your daughter or anyone else, would, if over a specified value rank for tax.

You will have noticed how statements about CTT bristle with

F

qualifications. It is one of the most complicated of all Inland Revenue enactments. It has caused more headaches and blood spitting than any other. CTT is a cumulative tax culminating at death in what used to be called Estate Duty (and which this new tax replaces). It is also a progressive tax, the rates increasing with the mounting total of taxable gifts. An odd feature is that the tax falls wholly on the giver and not at all on the receiver. In the eyes of the Inland Revenue it is more punishable to give than to receive. Fortunately for most people CTT hits hardest those who have a substantial surplus of possessions; there is something to be said for being poor! But in case of doubt it is worth seeking expert advice. Here, again, your bank manager should be able to help.

Taxation changes so rapidly that to give much detail here could become misleading before long. Ask your tax office and your bank manager for leaflets. Read the business sections of newspapers for comments on new legislation. Study your Tax Return Guide and keep it for reference after you have made your return.

We have considered your regular sources of earned income in retirement, mainly pensions and annuities. There may be casual or part-time earnings to provide a minor but useful supplement. If you have acquired one or two lump sums by chance or design, these have probably gone to swell your sources of unearned income.

INVESTMENT

Unearned or investment income is of two kinds. The great bulk of it is taxable. But there are small pockets of investment yielding a return which is tax free to help and encourage investment by the poorer nine-tenths of the community. Because of the administrative cost of discrimination, the concessions are available equally to the other tenth.

These are investments in certain National Savings. They include National Savings Bank ordinary accounts, index-linked Retirement Issue National Savings Certificates, and index-linked Save As You Earn. They are safe (the government guarantees the interest and the security of the capital sum) and simple (they are handled by the Post Office).

The National Savings Bank ordinary account is a utility. You can draw upon it for everyday expenses. Sums up to a limited amount can be drawn in cash on demand at any post office, and larger sums by post in the form of a warrant payable in cash at a post office, or a crossed warrant payable through your bank. The NSB is a convenient place to deposit spare cash. Deposits earn interest at a modest rate, but part of it – the amount is revised upwards from time to time – is free of all tax including Investment Income Surcharge.

Terms and facilities similar to those of the NSB are available at Trustee Savings Banks, but changes are planned.

NSB investment accounts give a higher rate of interest than deposits, but for that reason are less flexible. You have to give a month's notice of withdrawal, and all the interest is subject to income tax. Here the government is competing with other media of investment such as building societies, and you will have to decide which is the more convenient and profitable. Be sure that you are comparing like with like. NSB investment accounts pay the interest gross, but building societies pay net of tax at the standard rate. Since tax deducted at source by the building societies is not recoverable, non-taxpayers will probably find the NSB investment the better proposition.

There are other government investments which give good results for anyone who can afford to have money tied up for a period of years. One of these is Save as You Earn. As an index-linked form of saving the regular contributions have to be allowed to accumulate for the full five years' term in order to benefit from periodically calculated increases in the cost of living. In theory the cost of living can fall as well as rise, but we have not met anyone who would back that possibility. In any case you will not receive less than the total amount of your contribution. At the end of the term you can expect to receive your invested total upgraded to the new values.

Another medium for beating inflation is the National Savings Certificate. The comparatively new Retirement Issue for men aged sixty-five and women aged sixty and over are linked to the cost of living index. Husband and wife can each hold the maximum amount, in addition to other issues of National Savings Certificates. The retirement issue can be purchased in units, or multiples of units, or up to the permitted limit at one go. If held for a stated number of years they earn a tax-free bonus in addition to the inflation-proof advantage.

Savings Certificates other than index-linked issues increase by a fixed amount up to a declared maximum if held for a stated number of years. The increase in value is tax free. You can buy certificates up to the permitted maximum in any issue, irrespective of your holdings in previous issues.

Don't overlook any holdings you may have in earlier issues. They will continue to add small bonuses long after the term has expired, but these may not be the best return you can get on the money. It may be advisable to sell and put the proceeds into the latest issue of

Savings Certificates, or some other form of national savings such as British Savings Bonds.

New issues of British Savings Bonds are made from time to time at quite attractive interest rates. The bonds are purchased at £5 each and in multiples of £5 up to a maximum of £10 000. You will find details of these and other national savings in the Post Office Guide. There

Miraculously, a winning Premium Bond

should be a copy in your local reference library. For more particulars apply to the Department of National Savings at addresses given in the guide. Leaflets on the more popular forms of savings such as National Savings Bank and SAYE are available at any post office.

Premium Bonds are listed under national savings. Purely as a form of saving they rank with money hidden under the mattress. In effect they yield both less and more than other forms of national savings. They don't pay interest, but they can win you one of a range of tax-free prizes. You may get a nice little windfall, or a fortune, or nothing, according to the luck of the draw. There have been cases of a person's one and only bond scooping a substantial sum, but the odds are millions-to-one against. As you might expect, the more bonds you hold the bigger your chance of winning something. If you are prepared to freeze a few hundred pounds, Premium Bonds offer the safest kind of speculation. You can't lose your stake as in football pools or on the horses. If you can't afford the luxury of idle money, put your few hundreds in a building society.

Building societies are deservedly popular with small and with many not so small investors. They exist in all sizes, from giants like the Halifax and the Abbey National with vast funds and branches everywhere, to small societies with a local clientele. Make sure that the one you choose is a member of the Building Societies Association. That is a guarantee of safety for your money. It indicates that the handling of funds and mortgage policy conform to strict rules. The structure and procedures of building societies are laid down in a special Act of Parliament.

The hackneyed slogan 'safe as houses' applied to building societies is no exaggeration. If you invest a hundred pounds you will get a hundred pounds back whenever you choose to withdraw it. It may not be worth as much as when you paid it in, but that is because building society deposits and shares are not inflation-proof. Since they are not quoted securities they do not rise or fall with fluctuations in Stock Exchange values.

There is a limit to the amount of money you are permitted to hold in any one building society. It is currently £15 000. Husband and wife can each hold that maximum, and there is nothing to stop each from investing up to that limit in any number of building societies.

Interest rates paid to building society investors compare favourably with the return on other forms of investment. They are sensitive to general movements in interest rates and in the demand for houses. But changes are neither frequent nor extreme. A rise or fall is decided officially and announced well in advance. You usually get quite a long run at the going rate. You can leave the interest to be reinvested or have it paid to you half-yearly by warrant.

Though interest is paid net of income tax, non-taxpayers cannot claim a tax rebate. Moreover, for higher rate taxpayers the net return is subject to further tax deductions. Therefore investment in building societies may not be the most suitable for people paying less or more than the standard rate of income tax.

Investment in a building society is made easy. You don't need a broker or other intermediary in order to open and pay into an account. You can do this direct at any branch. If you have a share or deposit account you can also withdraw money easily; not always on demand as at your bank or the post office but at fairly short notice.

Competition among building societies is slight. Some societies offer a fractionally larger interest to investors, but otherwise the rates are uniform throughout the movement.

The societies are much alike in the choice of accounts offered. There are three main kinds. The ordinary account (sometimes divided into shares and deposits) is the most flexible, and appeals most to retired people. Regular savings schemes (often called subscription shares) are rewarded with a higher rate of interest, but they impose an obligation to keep up the contributions month after month. They are most suitable for people with a dependable earned income and reasonable assurance of a regular surplus.

There remains what is known as the term investment. If you have a lump sum that you can afford to tie up for one, two, three or more years, you can buy a building society bond. Interest at a higher rate than for shares and deposits is paid for the full term of the bond. A disadvantage is that you can't withdraw the sum before the end of the agreed term, unless you can prove exceptional need.

The safe and unexciting forms of investment we have described so far are for income rather than growth. There is an element of growth in index-linking, or if not growth in the fullest sense, at least non-shrinkage. These fairly high income schemes are recommended to senior citizens because most of them need income. Apart from index-linked, government-guaranteed schemes, you take a chance if you aim for growth.

Without being too pessimistic about the future one must recognize that growth in shares is largely for the young. They can look to a long future. But we need not rule out a little optimism. As we have pointed out repeatedly, men can live quite a long time after sixty-five, and women even longer. So inflation does matter. Investment income is a product of capital, and if capital is eroded income suffers too.

How to find growth without excessive risk is today's biggest investment problem. It is not for nothing that equities are known as risk capital. If you can't afford to lose, don't attempt to play the market. Even with a fair amount of knowledge you can get lost on the Stock Exchange. And these are baffling times for everybody.

If you want to risk an occasional plunge, test your hunch against some sober advice. Your portfolio may be too small for a stockbroker to bother with, but your bank manager will no doubt take the trouble. He will err on the side of caution. Remember, that the Stock Exchange offers no spectacular pickings for the small investor. Or for most big ones either.

Your portfolio may be too small for the stockbroker

You can find a measure of safety in equities by spreading the risk. The obvious way is through unit trusts. As you know, unit trusts hold a varied portfolio of shares, in which the managers make changes from time to time in accordance with their interpretation of trends. You will not make a fortune in unit trusts, but you are unlikely to lose disastrously. Since the trusts are based on variables, their own price fluctuates with the state of the market. But the spread of interests ensures that the rise and fall is never as extreme as it can be with an individual ordinary share.

Unit trusts are a long-term investment. If you are likely to need the money at short notice you may have to sell when the price is low. Ideally you should buy cheap, and be in a position to choose when to sell.

The units can be bought and sold direct or through your bank. The managers of the trust advertise special offers and new departures in newspapers, and include a coupon for easy response. They are obliged to insert in every advertisement a warning that prices of units and the income from them can go down as well as up.

As the name implies, the units are part of a trust fund. The trustees are usually a bank or an insurance company. Some banks operate their own unit trusts. Like the building societies, the unit trust movement is strictly controlled. The trustees have to enforce the rules laid down by the Department of Trade, ensure the efficiency and integrity of the managers, and protect the interests of unit holders.

It is a tribute to the strength of the movement that unit trusts have survived calamities that have hit their operators. There have been cases in recent years of conglomerates coming to grief without damage to the unit trusts in the group or loss to the unit holders.

Choosing a unit trust is not easy. The number and variety is bewildering. Most of them maintain a general portfolio with a wide mix of shares. In recent years the number of specialized trusts has increased, covering such fields as property, raw materials, commodities, new issues, and mining. Some specialize in foreign securities – American, Middle Eastern, Japanese.

This range of portfolios can be reduced to two broad classifications – income and growth. But even this simplification is deceptive. For instance, there are two sub-classes. One of these distinguishes between 'income' and 'high income' or 'extra income', according to the size of the yield. The other claims to combine income and growth. On what, then, do you base your choice?

First, you must make up your mind whether you want mainly income or mainly growth; or some of each and in what proportion. Next, you have to decide which are the most promising trusts in each category. There are published guides to unit trusts which can be helpful. Also, as in sport, you should study form. The financial press publishes lists periodically showing performance in the long and the short term within each category. These tell you what has happened, not what will happen. A past winner can become a loser. Apparently trivial political happenings or even a hint of possible trade union action can send the share barometer sharply up or down. But the experts are not much clearer than you are about long-term possibilities. Watch the trend and use your judgement.

Unit trust prices and yields are reported daily in the press. Two prices are quoted, bid and offer. The bid price is what you get if you sell; the offer, what you pay if you buy.

As with building society investment you can either draw the income or reinvest it. Some trusts offer accumulation units in which the dividend is automatically reinvested. Unit trusts enjoy a tax concession in the form of reduced CGT. The basic rate taxpayer may escape CGT altogether on the sale of his units.

As we have said, unit trusts should be regarded as a long-term investment. But there is no fixed term. You decide yourself when the time is ripe to sell, that is, you must be prepared to wait for the upturn or you will lose on the sale. That is true also of gilt-edged (i.e.

government) stocks except that these, for the most part, are dated and repayable at par on maturity.

Gilts are so-called for contrast with the more speculative ordinary industrial share. If you buy a stock with a par (i.e. face) value of £100 you will receive the full £100 at the redemption date. But in the meantime the price can fluctuate. If you need to sell when the market price has fallen below what you paid for the stock you can lose heavily. So think before you venture.

The interest on gilts is fixed and the rate may look poor, but that can be deceptive. It is the yield, not the interest, that matters when calculating the income from your investment. For instance, if the price of the stock when you buy is a quarter of the face value, the yield will be four times the fixed interest.

There is a further benefit. If you have bought at a favourable price and can wait for the stock to mature, you will gain on the redemption yield. And there is yet another advantage. Though the income is taxed like any other, your redemption profit will be exempt from CGT.

Local authority bonds are dated but generally for shorter periods than gilts. The term is fixed, but most authorities are willing to release the money on the death of the holder. The interest is fixed for the term of the loan, usually at quite a good rate.

These investments are popular especially with people who do not pay income tax. Tax is deductible at source, but the non-taxpayer can get a rebate, which is not possible with a building society. The sum invested is repaid in full on maturity.

Investing in a local authority is almost as uncomplicated as in a building society. You deal direct, and pay no brokerage or other charges. The authorities advertise the loan in small advertisements at the bottom of a column in the City pages of newspapers.

We have touched very superficially on the commonest forms of investment. The field is vast, and even a simple guide would fill a volume. Our concern however has been with the non-affluent and non-reckless retired person. The emphasis has been on income with some venturing into growth, and with as much certainty as these uncertain times can offer.

Where do we go from here?

In the last chapter you reviewed your retirement needs and estimated what you might be able to afford. Now, in the light of what we have discussed in the present chapter, you will reconsider your financial arrangements and see how far they meet the case. There may have to be some change of direction: how much more, and where, you should save; how you should redeploy stocks approaching redemption date.

Compare your own thoughts and practice with other people's. You may never have discussed money with your friends. It is a subject on which most of us are too reticent. But exchange of views need not be embarrassingly revealing. You may pick up a few ideas which you can try out on more expert advisers.

NEED FOR ADVICE

Be sure to seek professional advice. Your investment policy has probably been sound as far as it goes, but you may not be getting the best out of your money. The prospect of retirement adds a new and unfamiliar dimension. You need to consult someone who has dealt with many such cases.

If you do not employ a broker, or other investment specialist, or an accountant (and even if you do) speak to your bank manager. Bank facilities other than current and deposit accounts are not as widely known as they should be. Among them are investment management services and tax consultancy. If your financial resources are rather humble, and the money and tax problems of a kind that do not warrant a highly sophisticated service, don't on that account neglect making a date with your bank manager. His personal advice can clear up perplexities and help you to avoid pitfalls.

There is a further point to emphasize and that is the advisability of making your will. This applies equally to both spouses because a properly drawn will can avoid heartache and worry at what will already be a difficult time for the survivor.

Your bank manager or solicitor can explain how this can be arranged easily and at moderate cost. Unless you have professional experience it is best to resist the temptation of drawing a will yourself; it could cause more confusion than it seeks to avoid. As well as disposing of your assets in an orderly manner and in accordance with your wishes, a properly drawn will may mitigate taxation. Do choose your executor with care; a life-long friend for instance may outlive you by only a few months. It is preferable to consider the appointment of a professional adviser, such as your bank or solicitor. The professionals will charge your estate for their services and details of their current fees are readily available.

16
Countdown to R-Day

If you have drafted your plan more or less on the lines suggested, you have a self-portrait of a kind that will be new to you. It shows your life-pattern against the background of the things that make it possible. It is partly three-dimensional. The third dimension is a glimpse of how the pattern will adapt to a future in retirement.

Between now and retirement you will need to make those adaptations. They will have to be done in stages. The picture will not be quite the same in five years' time, and it will go on changing. There can be no finality till close to R-Day.

We have already advised annual updating to take account of variations in circumstances, financial and otherwise. But over and above this you need periodical policy reviews, perhaps at longer intervals, to consider the plan afresh and make radical changes if necessary. It is only too easy to regard the plan as final, and forget it. It is a working document, not an item in a filing cabinet.

So, let us start the count-down from the drafting date, ten years before retirement. Ten years feels, and undoubtedly is, a long time, even to people no longer in their first youth. You have ten more years of employment ahead. The world will change greatly in that decade. You realize this if you look back ten years and note how little of what has happened you could have foreseen. But don't be obsessed by the time factor. You started planning in order to counter the illusion that you had all the time in the world. And looking back you are aware of another phenomenon, how quickly the years have gone by.

One must be realistic. There *are* things you can't expect to make up your mind about ten years in advance. In fact, you have to keep an open mind, and an open plan, on most elements in the count. The word countdown suggests that there will be several stages, with second thoughts and modifications at each stage, and a little more certainty as we proceed.

The first stage, then, will come ten years before retirement, and the second stage, say five years later. Then it would be advisable to accelerate the process, with further reviews at three years, two years and one year before retirement.

Retirement minus ten years

At this distance from retirement you will be concerned largely with financial considerations. Money takes time to accumulate. Your concern will be to build up savings and therefore investment income.

Go over your checklist again. Decide what action is possible or desirable in each of the following main sections: assets — cash, savings, investments, house property, goods (including car and valuables); liabilities — mortgage, hire purchase, overdraft; income — earned and unearned; expenditure — household and personal.

If your job is secure you can look forward to a continuing earned income. Decide how much you can save and where to invest it. Look at your existing investments. Are you getting the best out of them? Which of them have growth potential? Check up on your insurances and dated stocks and bonds, and decide what to do with money that is repayable within a year or two.

Look to your debts and how to phase them out. Perhaps now is the time to start using cash instead of credit for further commitments. Time also to scrutinize further commitments, with retirement priorities as well as present interests in mind.

Have you still got the pension booklet your firm handed you many years ago, together with all subsequent amendments? Ask for a replacement if you have mislaid it. Read it again, and seek enlightenment on anything you don't understand.

Retirement minus five years

Much has changed in these five years. Some of your assumptions may have been proved wrong. Some plans may have to be scrapped, others improved or developed along new lines. The time has come for an overall revision.

What is your money position? How much have you saved? Is it enough? Can you save more? Which of your investments look better — worse — no different — after five years? Has your income from all sources kept level with inflation? Or has it moved ahead, or slipped back, and by how much?

What has happened to your living standard? Have you cut down on entertainment and other personal and household expenditure, and have you any regrets? It is difficult to reduce expenditure in absolute terms while the cost of living is rising generally, but you can reduce your proportionate costs.

Has your health changed? Perhaps you should look for ways of taking the hard labour out of gardening. If you have had twinges of back trouble you might decide to invest in an orthopaedic bed, or a new bath with hand grips. These things will be useful now as well as later, and you may not be able to afford them after retirement. Are there any other gaps in your equipment which would be worth filling before prices go higher?

In addition to gaps there may be redundancies. You must have made an inventory for insurance purposes. Look at it now, bring it up to date, and decide what you can unload. Some of the goods are lumber, mere space-fillers for which you may not have space in retirement. Some may have sales value. Decide whether to turn them into cash now, or regard them as a capital reserve to be sold when the market is favourable or the need arises.

Would you keep your house or move? If to move, where and into what kind of accommodation? The pros and cons have to be debated some years before retirement, and perhaps retirement minus five years is the time to begin. Don't mark time on house improvements meanwhile. These will increase its value if you decide to sell. Besides, you may want to stay. No decision need be final. Any proposal is subject to revision or reversal under pressure from events.

Retirement minus three years

The procedure, initially, will be much as before. Review your financial position and make any new dispositions that you think suitable. Professional advice is specially worth having at this late stage.

How have the cuts in personal and household expenditure worked out? How has your life style changed? Are you happy with the result? Have you carried austerity too far? Do a little subjective stock-taking in co-operation with your wife.

You might start some modest stockpiling for your retirement. Not foodstuffs, even in tins. Space is limited and you are not preparing for a siege. There are, however, some semi-durables which are easier to buy out of occupational earnings than out of retirement income. They include clothing, bed linen, furnishings and other fabrics.

Household linen presents no special problems. If you are keeping your house you might want to renew curtains and carpets, and renovate and re-cover any furniture not earmarked for sale or jumble. Look over your wardrobe. See that you have enough suits, leisure wear and under-wear before even sales prices become prohibitive.

Women's clothes are not so easy to stock up. Styles don't last. But some garments, not exclusively the ones out of sight, are ageless, as every woman knows. Add a few warm items to the list.

If you have not calculated the cost of running your car, do it now. Estimate how much less it would cost in the more restricted life of retirement. What would you save now if you traded your car in for a smaller, more economical one? If you have a company car, would it be feasible to buy it when you retire and get rid of your own? On the other hand, will you really need a car or want to drive once you have retired? Will you be able to afford it anyway? These are big decisions, and three years from retirement day is not too soon to start thinking.

Retirement minus two years

Check the whole plan as you did a year ago: income and expenditure, savings and investment, your way of life and how and why it has changed; and in particular your occupational pension.

If as seems likely the company pension will be based on your last three years' salary, you can now calculate what you will get. Read the conditions again, and if there have been changes make sure you under-stand how they affect you. Have a talk with whoever is concerned about the firm's pension commuting policy. You are near enough to retirement to work out the economics of taking part of your entitle-ment in a lump sum.

Have you decided whether to keep your house or move? If to move, you will be studying the property market, and will have made the kind of enquiries suggested in Chapter 11. If you are seriously thinking of living abroad you will be undergoing deeper heart searchings, and studying geography, climate, politics, exchange regulations, and living costs and conditions in the territory.

If you have decided to stay where you are, look at your house from the point of view of a retirement home. Is it warm enough? Are the insulation and draught-proofing adequate? It might be wise to get a builder to look over the structure for any defects or deterioration that

Studying geography and climate (with a view to settling abroad)

will be cheaper to correct now than in a couple of years time. It is a good idea to have the place decorated throughout. That means the outside too. Unless you are as good as the professionals (be honest with yourself) and don't feel uneasy on a ladder, get the best contractor you know to do the job. It won't be cheap, but it will be dearer if you delay. The new look won't last right through your retirement, but it will give you a good start. And it may make all the difference if you change your mind and decide to sell the house after all.

Retirement minus one year

This is virtually the final check-up on your money before retirement makes a radical change in your circumstances. The date is near enough to make a reasonable estimate of what your net income will be.

Set down your present gross income from all sources, apart from employment income. Add the pension income to come. Deduct income tax, taking into account all allowances, on the basis of the latest legislation. The figure will not be exact, but it will be near enough for you to start preparing your retirement budget. It will also indicate whether you need to look for a further source of earned income in retirement.

If you have decided to commute your pension, you will have a lump sum which you can invest for income. So you will if you sell your house and buy a smaller one or rent an apartment. Will you have enough to live on and provide a safety margin? Retirement will reduce your expenditure in ways which were explained in the last two chapters. You have probably made further economies through changes in your way of life and cutting out what you have felt to be extravagances. You may still want a paid part-time retirement job, for the pleasure as well as the pay.

Now is the time to explore the possibilities. You may be fortunate enough to line something up before you retire. At least you will have time to pick and choose. If you have a side-line already, you can be thinking of ways to develop it.

Make a point of briefing yourself on the tax position of retired people. We have referred to some special provisions, but changes may be taking place while this book is being printed. Find out also about travel and other age concessions. They will affect your retirement budgeting.

Your employer may well have a Pensioners' Association or a Pensioners' Welfare Officer. The year before retirement is an appropriate time to consult them on the problems and privileges of retired members.

This countdown is not a prescription but a suggestion. No one can tell you what to do in detail. You will make your own calculations and comparisons, and vary the method to suit your circumstances. As with every stage of the pre-retirement plan, all we can do is to offer what we hope is a useful frame for your own individual picture.

17

A Retirement Budget

Three chapters ago you asked a question, 'What shall I be able to afford when I retire?' We don't pretend that we have found you the complete answer. There are no certainties even in the best-laid plans. But this one should not go wildly awry. It has shown due regard for the unpredictables in life and in the national economy. It has been definite only about those matters which lend themselves to definition.

What has the plan done for you? It has set down your capital of all kinds and your income from all sources. It has made you examine your portfolio to determine how it would fit a retirement economy and what improvements were desirable. It has given you a detailed account of your expenditure, and has balanced outgoings against income. You may have had no doubts about your solvency, but the plan has told you something about your efficiency.

By marshalling facts and tracing inter-relations, the plan has had a steadying influence. With retirement in the middle distance it has weighed up the relative merits of growth and income from investment. You have been careful not to tie up capital further ahead than prudence would recommend. You have come down on the side of caution when tempted to speculate. In short, you have faced the financial realities of retirement.

There have been other gains. You have watched how your way of life has changed, partly under the compulsions of age, but also deliberately in preparation for retirement. You have been able to equate this changing pattern of living with the changing value of money. Your personal audit revealed facts about yourself to prepare you for the emotional shock of retirement. The financial audit has helped to reassure you that adjustment to retirement is an exercise in management, not acceptance of defeat.

A planned retirement has underlined priorities in money management and living standards. It has made you aware of the distinction between essentials and expendables, between needs and wants. It has pin-pointed areas where waste can occur through ignorance, and shown that economies can be achieved without deprivation.

Not the least important effect of the plan has been to give you a more accurate measure of inflation. The official figures are too abstract to be helpful at the level of household and personal spending. But your experience of increasing costs is beyond dispute. The experts may say that inflation is running at a given percentage, and in the abstract they may be right. But if your expenditure is higher than that of the previous year, you know more than the pundits about the one case that matters.

At the final countdown in the last chapter you estimated what your net income would be in retirement. The estimate will be near enough for budgeting purposes. Some of your income is probably reinvested, either by your own wish or under the terms of the investment. In the former case you can draw it whenever you wish; in the latter you will have to wait till the redemption date of the stock. Some income may be fixed in amount, such as that from local government loans, and of course your occupational pension if it is not index-linked. Some may or may not remain unchanged, viz. annuities, in which the interest element varies with changes in income tax, and the state pension which the Chancellor of the Exchequer raises at his discretion. Paid work may yield a variable income; so will unit trusts, equities, and anything which is dependent on Stock Exchange fluctuations. Your budget will make allowance for the variations.

With a not very serious margin of error, you can know the net income upon which to base the year's budget. You know how far your pensions fall short of your former salary. You have increased your income from investments by your savings. You may in fact be no poorer than you were before retirement. That would be exceptional. The likelihood is that your total income is lower and that you know by how much. Somehow you must make a proportionate reduction in your expenditure.

We shall assume that you have paid off your long-term debts — mortgage, overdraft, hire purchase. You are concerned to make ends meet out of income during the year, and leave a reasonable margin for contingencies.

Some expenses, such as rent (if any) and rates, are known to you in advance and are therefore easy to allow for. Insurance premiums will no doubt have to be higher than last year's. Service charges for equipment may rise, and replacement of parts owing to wear or breakdown are unpredictable. The television hire charge may be increased; so may the telephone rental, though you can control your total expenditure on calls. Otherwise you can't do anything to reduce those costs, short of giving up the television, which would be a pity, and the telephone, which would be very unwise.

How much warmth is enough?

Heating is another matter. The costs will vary according to the length and severity of the winter, and the degree of control the system permits. You can't predict how much warmth will be enough. The best you can do is to look at last year's bills and add a percentage for inflation and arbitrary charges. If you find you have overestimated the increase, you can give yourself a bonus. If you have actually saved on last year you can believe in miracles.

More flexible than heating are the housekeeping expenses. Beyond a certain point they are what you choose to make them. As we have seen, your way of living has changed during the planning period. You know what you can do without. You can distinguish between necessities and luxuries. Whatever else is sacrificed, continue to eat well. According to a recent survey by Age Concern, even the more affluent retired spend the largest proportion of their money on food.

Food and materials are among the most difficult items to budget. They are less so if you have kept an account of your spending on these items as part of your plan. Look at last year's record, strike out what you think you can dispense with, put a query against those you will retain if you can afford them, then total the cost of what remains, and update it for the new budget.

One of the queries will be against 'meals out'. These have risen in price more steeply than almost any other form of indulgence. And expense accounts have ceased with the job. You will have to make ad hoc decisions. For most of us eating at home is expensive enough.

So far the budget has not offered much scope for reducing expenditure. Such savings as you have made could be balanced or even exceeded by the rise in the cost of living. Only if you have moved into smaller accommodation will you be spending less, absolutely as well as relatively, on heating for instance and rates.

Otherwise, the biggest lump saving can be made on the car. You have decided whether to keep your present vehicle, or to exchange it for a smaller car, or to do without. Whatever your choice, you have to estimate what you can afford to spend on travel. Concessions on public transport will help to cut the cost, but by how much? You can only guess. Any figure you put down will bear only the most tenuous relation to last year's. Railway fares will be costly even for privileged retired people, and car hire may become a rare necessity rather than an occasional luxury.

There are two ways of budgeting for holidays. You can choose the location and the kind of accommodation wanted, and decide whether you can afford the likely cost; or you can allocate a sum and decide to keep reasonably within that limit. The second way is for the not so well-to-do. Like every budget decision it is not inflexible. You may have saved enough elsewhere to extend your stay, go further afield than at first contemplated, or enjoy better accommodation. The budgeted figure is a guide only.

Your social life may have changed with the years, but you will not become a hermit in retirement. You will still try to afford the little goodwill offerings you take when visiting friends. With those in your own class and circumstances you will probably develop an unspoken agreement on where to draw the line. It is impossible to predict the number and likely cost of social obligations. Make a guess, with some reference to past experience. Christmas is easier. Since it comes but once a year, budget generously for your family and friends. The year will be near its end, and if you have estimated well on everything else you should have the necessary surplus.

Recreations are another flexible category. Since they occur at intervals and do not singly involve a large outlay, you can decide to indulge or not, as they come. A budget, however, demands an estimated overall figure, and you can base this on last year's activities. The figure can be in the same proportion as this year's income is to your immediate pre-retirement income, with an adjustment for inflation. It will allow for sport, club subscriptions, entertainments, reading, garden and other leisure activities.

Some normal expenditure will have been forestalled by your prudence in stocking up and by the change in circumstances. Clothing will have been largely taken care of, except for cleaning and laundering. The house, we suppose, is in good enough decorative condition. In any case, you can look at it with half closed eyes and say it will do for another year.

The remaining category, pocket money, is the least calculable of all. In an earlier chapter we advised setting aside a weekly allowance for personal spending. If you remember the amount and how it worked out, and take into account changed needs and tastes, you can apply the method again. It is better than leaving the oddments of spending to chance and wondering where the money has gone.

Budgeting becomes easier with time. You revise the last one upwards or downwards in accordance with changed circumstances. Indeed, a pre-retirement budget is facilitated by all the planning that has gone before. One of the major benefits of the plan is that it helps you as it were to enter upon retirement by degrees.

We must emphasize again that you need not make heavy weather of the plan or the budget. Few of us are, or would want to be, accountants and auditors in private life. But we all need to know our financial position and to feel we are in control. Any little approach towards certainty means that much avoidance of stress.

If the outline budget above seems preoccupied with economy, this is not in expectation of an austere life in retirement. It has a much more hopeful purpose. First, to encourage a realistic attitude to the new life. Second, to identify and accept its priorities. Third, to live comfortably within one's means, whatever they may be. And fourth, to achieve a satisfying as well as a solvent retirement.

Appendix

Addresses of organizations: Yellow Pages classified telephone directory; post office; public library.

(Headquarters' addresses below are correct at the time of going to press. Enquire whether you have a local branch.)

General information and advice: local Citizens' Advice Bureau; Pre-Retirement Association, 19 Undine Street, London SW17 (01–767 3225); your former employer's Pensioners' Association or Pensioners' Welfare Officer.

Voluntary work: Women's Royal Voluntary Service, 17 Old Park Lane, London W1Y 4AS (01–499 6040); National Council of Social Service, 26 Bedford Square, London WC1 (01–636 4066); Age Concern, Bernard Sunley House, 60 Pitcairn Road, Mitcham, Surrey (01–640 5431); Help the Aged, 8 Denman Street, London, W1 (01–437 2554); local hospital; church.

Paid work: local newspaper; The Employment Fellowship, Drayton House, Gordon Street, London WC1 (01–387 1828); Success After Sixty, 14 Great Castle Street, London W1 (01–580 8932).

Education: public library notice board; local council education department; local college of further education; the Open University, PO Box 48, Milton Keynes, Bucks. MK7 6AB.

Pensions: local office of the Department of Health and Social Security.

Taxation: local tax office.

Savings and investment: post office; your bank manger.

SOME USEFUL PUBLICATIONS

Choice, the magazine of the Pre-Retirement Association. Available from the PRA or from newsagents.

Money Which?, periodical published by the Consumers' Association, 14 Buckingham Street, London WC2N 6DS (01–839 1222).

Income Tax and the Elderly IR 4; *Taxation of Wife's Earnings* IR 13; *Income Tax and Widows* IR 23: all from your tax office.

Retirement Pensions NI 15; *Retirement Pensions for Widows* NI 15A; *Retirement Benefits for Married Women* NI 15B; *Guidance for the Self-Employed* NI 41; *Cancelling Retirement and Earning an Increased Pension* NI 92; and other leaflets from your local DHSS office.

Investing in National Savings, National Savings for You, and leaflets on individual savings schemes from post offices or the National Savings Movement headquarters.

The Management of Your Investments: The Portfolio Investment Fund; National Westminster Unit Trusts; Budget Account; Executor and Trustee Services: from branches of the National Westminster Bank.

Guide to the Social Services: *Voluntary Social Services Directory and Handbook*: *Charities Digest*: at public reference libraries.

Index

warmth, 72, 120–1
weight loss, 82
weight problems, 56–61, 65
wine-making, 106
wives and retirement, 20–1, 28, 41, 101–2, 115
Women's Institutes, 98–9, 102, 107

Women's Royal Voluntary Service (WRVS), 100, 122–3
working retirment, 83–92
writing, 34, 107

younger people, mixing with, 51–3